Dandelion Book
High Frequency Words

Spelling, Comprehension and Games
Resource Book for KS1
Complements Dandelion Books
Units 1-20

PhonicBooks™

© Phonic Books Ltd 2013.

Contents

Introduction	page 4
High-frequency words pupil record sheet	page 6
High-frequency word - reading cards	page 7
High-frequency word - writing cards	page 133
This folder belongs to	page 10
Lesson 1 - Unit 1 a, I, is, it	page 11
Lesson 2 - Unit 2 the, not, is, on	page 15
Lesson 3 - Unit 3 his, has, can, the	page 21
Lesson 4 - Unit 4 he, be, me, of	page 27
Lesson 5 - Unit 5 for, to, put, but	page 33
Lesson 6 - Unit 6 have, put, was, for	page 39
Lesson 7 - Unit 7 you, was, said, off	page 45
Lesson 8 - Unit 8 don't, say, puts, and	page 51
Lesson 9 - Unit 9 do, says, from, are	page 57
Lesson 10 - Unit 10 don't, says, love, my	page 63
Lesson 11 - Unit 11 such, we, see, her	page 69
Lesson 12 - Unit 12 she, wish, give, live	page 75
Lesson 13 - Unit 13 this, that, they, with	page 81
Lesson 14 - Unit 14 no, go, so, old	page 87
Lesson 15 - Unit 15 long, along, going, think	page 93
Lesson 16 - Unit 16 loves, have, lives, gives	page 99
Lesson 17 - Unit 17 what, why, who, where	page 105
Lesson 18 - Unit 18 looked, into, asked, stopped	page 115
Lesson 19 - Unit 19 too, all, by, began	page 121
Lesson 20 - Unit 20 once, oh, one, there	page 127

Dandelion book of high-frequency words

Who is this workbook for?

Many common words (high-frequency words) that beginner readers need to learn have complex spellings. Some children will move up into year 1 experiencing difficulties reading and/or spelling these high-frequency words. This workbook offers spelling and comprehension exercises and reading games which will help children learn to read and spell these words.

What is the aim of the comprehension sheets?

The aim is to work with the words in a multi-sensory way by reading them, breaking them up into sounds and writing them. This way, the pupil is encouraged to use the synthetic phonic approach of segmenting words into their sounds, even with words that have complex spellings.

Once the learners have read and written the four words in the box at the top of the comprehension worksheets, they have to read the sentences and insert the correct word. The exercises will help the learners internalise the recognition and the spelling of the words.

If the teacher feels the learner needs further multi-sensory activity before doing the worksheet, other possible activities could be making the words using rolled out plasticene, drawing the words in a tray of sand using his/her finger, doing rainbow writing (we have provided words for this at the back of this workbook) and/or wordbuilding the words using wooden or plastic letters.

What is the rationale behind the high-frequency words chosen?

The gradual introduction of high-frequency words matches the progression in the Dandelion Launchers and Dandelion Readers reading scheme, initially only introducing letters at the level of the corresponding Unit. Many of the vowel sounds in the words will not have been covered by the learner at that stage and he/she will need to have this explained to them. The sounds and spellings which the pupil may find difficult are listed at the bottom of each comprehension sheet.

Sometimes a high-frequency word has been repeated in another lesson. From our experience of teaching children with learning difficulties, we have found that revisiting is often the way forward to help them internalise the reading and spelling of the words.

The words chosen for the lesson are in a box at the top of the comprehension sheet. The pupil must write the words saying the sounds as he/she writes them. The learner will need to understand early on that a sound can sometimes be represented by more than one letter and that a letter can represent more than one sound.

The learners will have to read the sentences one at a time and decide which word needs to be added so that the sentence makes sense.

There are two different sheets for each set of four words. A third sheet gives the answers to help the teacher.

High-frequency words cards

Small reading cards have been provided at the front of the workbook on page ..., so that the teacher can use these to test the child's knowledge out of the context of sentences. These can be photocopied and laminated. A larger version has also been provided at the beginning of each lesson for those children who would benefit from looking at a larger version of the word. It is recommended that these be used after the learners have had experience reading and writing these words using the activities described above.

The two games

The games are to help with the recognition and the reading of the chosen high-frequency words.

The first game only has the four words relating to that lesson, in random order.

The second game is 4-in-a-Row. This game incorporates the new words, whilst providing revision of words from previous lessons. The aim has been to keep using some of the more challenging words from past lessons to help with consolidation.

Record sheet

A tick sheet has been included for the teacher to make notes and keep a record of a pupil's progress.

PUPIL RECORD FOR HIGH-FREQUENCY WORDS

Name: Date:

	✓		✓		✓	NOTES
Lesson 1	a	I	is	it		
Lesson 2	the	not	is	on		
Lesson 3	his	has	can	the		
Lesson 4	he	be	me	of		
Lesson 5	for	to	put	but		
Lesson 6	have	put	was	for		
Lesson 7	you	was	said	off		
Lesson 8	don't	say	puts	and		
Lesson 9	do	says	from	are		
Lesson 10	don't	says	love	my		
Lesson 11	such	we	see	her		
Lesson 12	she	wish	give	live		
Lesson 13	this	that	they	with		
Lesson 14	no	go	so	old		
Lesson 15	long	along	going	think		
Lesson 16	loves	have	lives	gives		
Lesson 17	what	why	who	where		
Lesson 18	looked	into	asked	stopped		
Lesson 19	too	all	by	began		
Lesson 20	once	oh	one	there		

This page may be photocopied by the purchaser. © Phonic books Ltd 2013.

Units 1 - 20
High-frequency words (1)

a	I	is
it	the	not
on	his	has
can	he	be
me	of	for
to	put	but
have	was	you
said	off	don't
say	puts	and

Cards to help children read and write high-frequency words with complex spellings.
This sheet may be photocopied by the purchaser. © Phonic Books Ltd 2013.

Units 1 – 20
High-frequency words (2)

do	says	from
are	love	my
such	we	see
her	she	wish
give	live	this
that	they	with
no	go	so
old	long	along
going	think	loves

Cards to help children read and write high-frequency words with complex spellings.
This sheet may be photocopied by the purchaser. © Phonic Books Ltd 2013.

Units 1 - 20
High-frequency words (3)

lives	have	gives
what	why	who
where	looked	into
asked	stopped	too
all	by	began
once	one	oh
there		

Cards to help children read and write high-frequency words with complex spellings.
This sheet may be photocopied by the purchaser. © Phonic Books Ltd 2013.

Dandelion Book of High-frequency Words

This book belongs to

This sheet may be photocopied by the purchaser. © Phonic Books Ltd 2011

Lesson 1 – Unit 1

a

I

is

it

Unit 1 - Find the word

a __	I __
is __ __	it __ __

1. __ am Tam.

2. __ __ is Sam.

3. __ am Tim.

4. "Sam, __ __ is __ mat."

5. __ am __ mat.

6. "Tam, it __ __ a mat."

7. __ am Sam.

8. It __ __ a mat.

9. "Tim, __ __ is __ mat."

Unit 1 spellings of high-frequency words, some of which have complex spellings: a, I, is, it. Explain to the learner that the letter <i> in the word <I> represents the sound /ie/ and the letter <s> in the word <is> represents the sound /z/. Make sure the writer says the sounds as he/she writes the word. This sheet may be photocopied by the purchaser. © Phonic Books Ltd 2013.

Unit 1 - Find the word - Teacher's sheet

a *a*	I *I*
is *i s*	it *i t*

1. *I* am Tam.

2. *It* is Sam.

3. *I* am Tim.

4. "Sam, *it* is *a* mat."

5. *I* am *a* mat.

6. "Tam, it *is* a mat."

7. *I* am Sam.

8. It *is* a mat.

9. "Tim, *it* is *a* mat."

Unit 1 spellings of high-frequency words, some of which have complex spellings: a, I, is, it. Explain to the learner that the letter <i> in the word <I> represents the sound /ie/ and the letter <s> in the word <is> represents the sound /z/. Make sure the writer says the sounds as he/she writes the word. This sheet may be photocopied by the purchaser. © Phonic Books Ltd 2013.

Lesson 1
Stepping Stones game

start

finish

This game is for 1–4 players. Play with counters and die. This sheet may be photocopied by the purchaser. © Phonic Books Ltd. 2013.

Lesson 2 - Unit 2

the

not

is

on

Unit 2 - Find the word (1)

the ____ __	not __ __ __
is __ __	on __ __

1. Pam __ __ in the pot.

2. The pin is __ __ __ on the mat.

3. Pip __ __ on ____ __ mop.

4. ____ __ tin is on ____ __ top.

5. Sam is __ __ __ on the mat.

Unit 2 spellings of high-frequency words, some of which have complex spellings: is, not, on, the. Explain that the sound /th/ is represented by two letters in the word <the>. Explain that the letter <s> in the word <is> represents the sound /z/. Make sure the learner can write the letters <h> and <e> before doing this sheet. Make sure the writer says the sounds as he/she writes the words. This sheet may be photocopied by the purchaser. © Phonic Books Ltd 2013.

Unit 2 - Find the word (2)

the ____ __	not __ __ __
is __ __	on __ __

1. ____ __ map __ __   __ __ __ on the mat.

2. "____ __ tap is __ __, Pip!"

3. Pam __ __ on top.

4. "Tom, ____ __ map is __ __ the mat."

5. "__ __ __ in ____ __ pot, Pam!"

Unit 2 spellings of high-frequency words, some of which have complex spellings: is, not, on, the. Explain that the sound /th/ is represented by two letters in the word ‹the›. Explain that the letter ‹s› in the word ‹is› represents the sound /z/. Make sure the learner can write the letters ‹h› and ‹e› before doing this sheet. Make sure the writer says the sounds as he/she writes the words. This sheet may be photocopied by the purchaser. © Phonic Books Ltd 2013.

Unit 2 - Find the word - Teacher's sheet

the	_th_ e	not	_n_ _o_ _t_
is	_i_ _s_	on	_o_ _n_

Sheet 1

1. Pam _is_ in the pot.

2. The pin is _not_ on the mat.

3. Pip _is_ on _the_ mop.

4. The tin _is_ on _the_ top.

5. Sam is _not_ on the mat.

Sheet 2

1. _The_ map _is_ _not_ on the mat.

2. "_The_ tap is on, Pip!"

3. Pam _is_ on top.

4. "Tom, _the_ map is _on_ the mat."

5. "_Not_ in _the_ pot, Pam!"

Unit 2 spellings of high-frequency words, some of which have complex spellings: is, not, on, the. Explain that the sound /th/ is represented by two letters in the word <the>. Explain that the letter <s> in the word <is> represents the sound /z/. Make sure the learner can write the letters <h> and <e> before doing this sheet. Make sure the writer says the sounds as he/she writes the words. This sheet may be photocopied by the purchaser. © Phonic Books Ltd 2013.

Lesson 2
Stepping Stones game

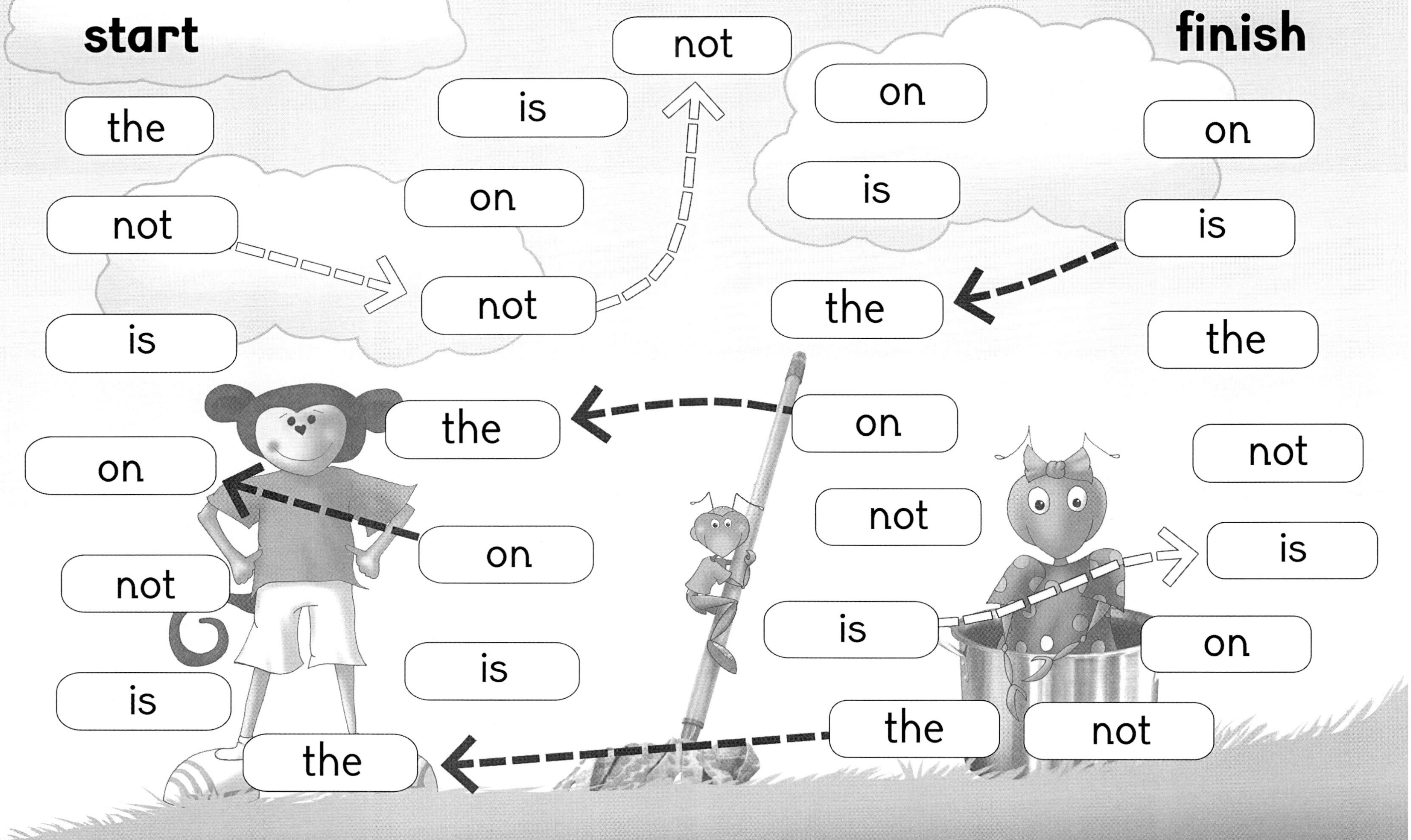

start — the, not, is, on, not, is, the, on, is, the

finish — on, is, the, not, is, on, not, is, the, on, not, is, the

This game is for 1–4 players. Play with counters and die. This sheet may be photocopied by the purchaser. © Phonic Books Ltd. 2013.

4-in-a-Row Game - Unit 2

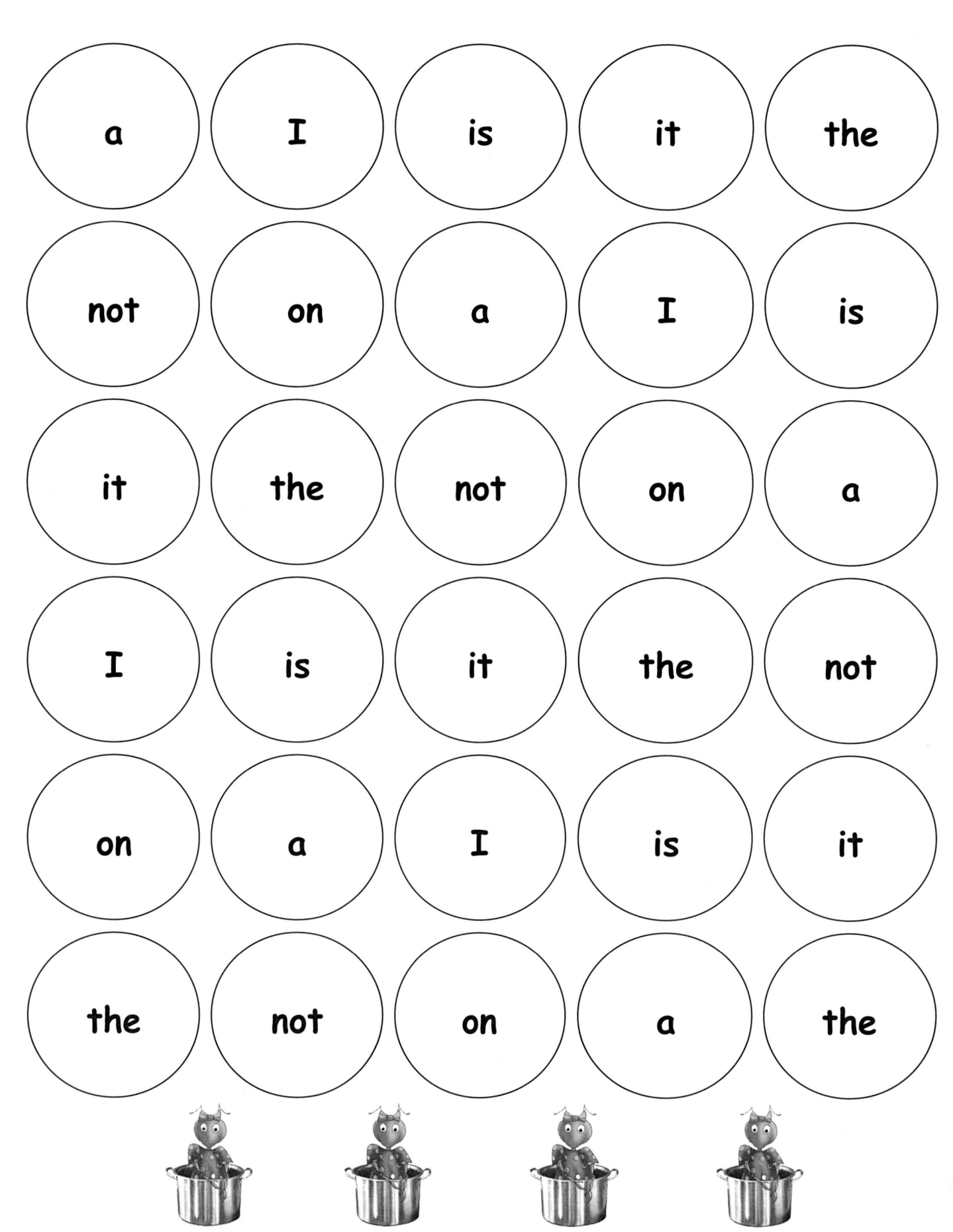

a	I	is	it	the
not	on	a	I	is
it	the	not	on	a
I	is	it	the	not
on	a	I	is	it
the	not	on	a	the

Two different sets of coloured counters are needed. Two players take it in turns to read the word and put a counter on the word. The winner is the first to get four counters in a row. Play four games. When a game is won, the winner places a counter on the picture at the bottom of the page. This sheet may be photocopied by the purchaser. © Phonic Books Ltd 2013.

Lesson 3 - Unit 3

his

has

can

the

Unit 3 - Find the word (1)

his ___ ___ ___	has ___ ___ ___
can ___ ___ ___	the ___ ___ ___

1. Pip ___ ___ ___ a cap.

2. ___ ___ ___ cap is on ___ ___ ___ bag.

3. Pam ___ ___ ___ get the bag.

4. Pam ___ ___ ___ a big sob.

5. Pip ___ ___ ___ got ___ ___ ___ cat.

Unit 3 spellings of high-frequency words, some of which have complex spellings: his, has, can, the. Explain that the sound /th/ in the word <the> is represented by two letters. Explain that in the words <his, has> the <s> represents the sound /z/. Make sure the writer says the sounds as he/she writes the words. This sheet may be photocopied by the purchaser. © Phonic Books 2013.

Unit 3 - Find the word (2)

his __ __ __	has __ __ __
can __ __ __	the __ __ __

1. Pip has __ __ __ bat.

2. Pip __ __ __ not hit it.

3. Pip __ __ __ a big pan.

4. Pip has __ __ __ big pan.

5. Pip __ __ __ hit it.

BAM!

Unit 3 spellings of high-frequency words, some of which have complex spellings: his, has, can, the. Explain that the sound /th/ in the word <the> is represented by two letters. Explain that in the words <his, has> the <s> represents the sound /z/. Make sure the writer says the sounds as he/she writes the words. This sheet may be photocopied by the purchaser. © Phonic Books 2013.

24 Unit 3 - Find the word - Teacher's sheet

| his _h i s_ | has _h a s_ |
| can _c a n_ | the _th e_ |

Sheet 1

1. Pip _has_ a cap.

2. _His_ cap is on _the_ bag.

3. Pam _can_ get the bag.

4. Pam _has_ a big sob.

5. Pip _has_ got _the_ cat.

Sheet 2

1. Pip has _the_ bat.

2. Pip _can_ not hit it.

3. Pip _has_ a big pan.

4. Pip has _his_ big pan.

5. Pip _can_ hit it.

Unit 3 spellings of high-frequency words, some of which have complex spellings: his, has, can, the. Explain that the sound /th/ in the word ‹the› is represented by two letters. Explain that in the words ‹his, has› the ‹s› represents the sound /z/. Make sure the writer says the sounds as he/she writes the words. This sheet may be photocopied by the purchaser. © Phonic Books 2013.

Lesson 3
Stepping Stones game

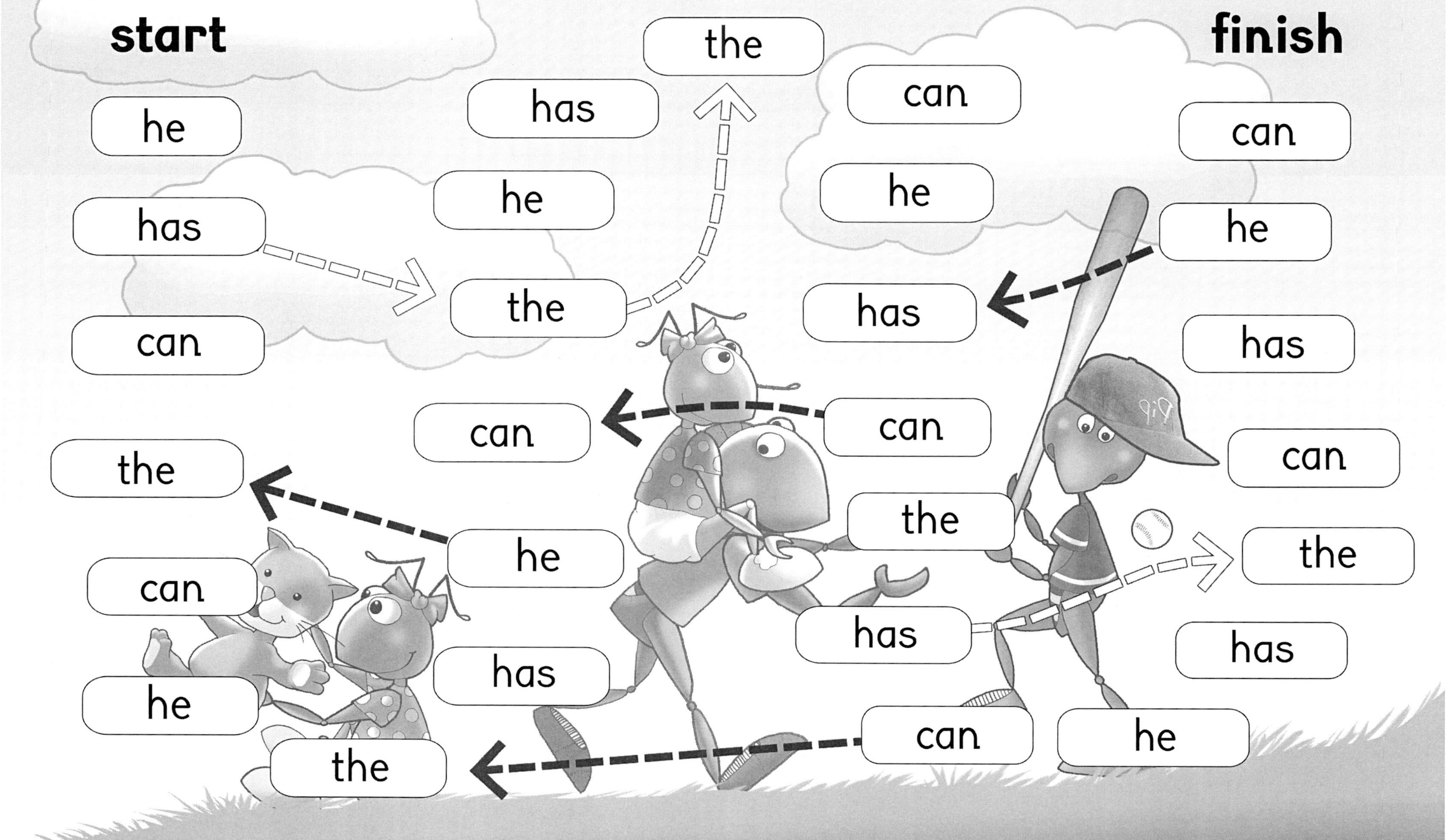

start → he → has → can → the → he → can → the → has → he → can → has → the → can → the → has → he → can → has → he → can → he → has → the → **finish**

This game is for 1–4 players. Play with counters and die. This sheet may be photocopied by the purchaser. © Phonic Books Ltd. 2013.

4-in-a-Row Game - Unit 3

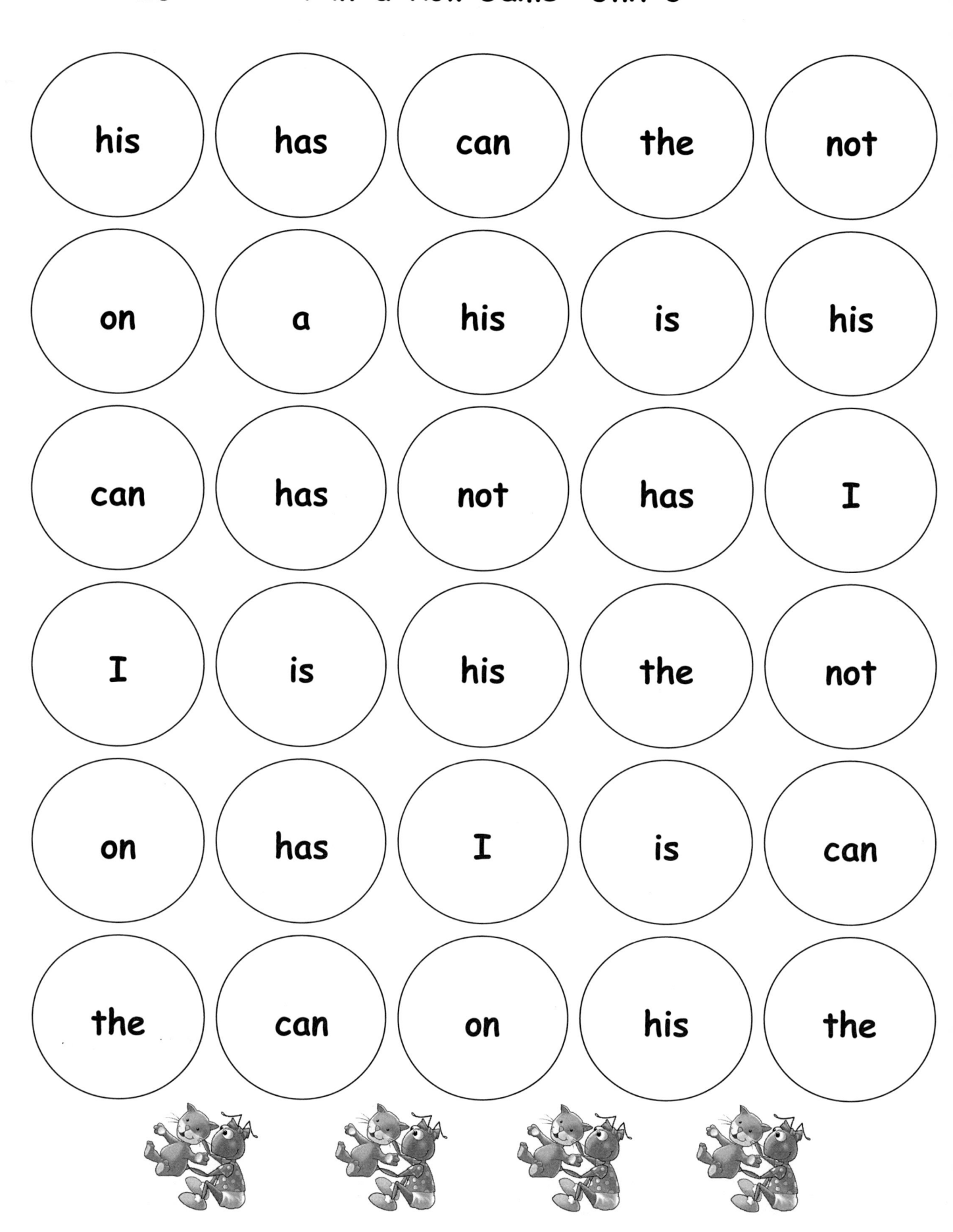

his	has	can	the	not
on	a	his	is	his
can	has	not	has	I
I	is	his	the	not
on	has	I	is	can
the	can	on	his	the

Two different sets of coloured counters are needed. Two players take it in turns to read the word and put a counter on the word. The winner is the first to get four counters in a row. Play four games. When a game is won, the winner places a counter on the picture at the bottom of the page. This sheet may be photocopied by the purchaser. © Phonic Books Ltd 2013.

Lesson 4 – Unit 4

he

be

me

of

Unit 4 - Find the word (1)

he __ __	be __ __
me __ __	of __ __

1. "Dan can __ __ the Dad."

2. __ __ can __ __ the Dad.

3. "Get __ __ a map, Viv."

4. "Tam can __ __ a vet."

5. Tam fed Bob a bit __ __ cod.

6. Bob, the cat is sad. __ __ can not fit as __ __ is fat.

Unit 4 spellings of high-frequency words, some of which have complex spellings: he, be, me, of. Explain that in the words <he, be, me> the letter <e> has the /ee/ sound and that the letter <f> in the word <of> represents the /v/ sound. Make sure the writer says the sounds as he/she writes the words. This sheet may be photocopied by the purchaser. © Phonic Books Ltd 2013.

Unit 4 - Find the word (2)

he __ __	be __ __
me __ __	of __ __

1. Tam can __ __ the Mum.

2. "Get __ __ a peg, Ted."

3. Dan fed Bob a pot __ __ cod.

4. "Pip, get __ __ the fan on the bed."

5. __ __ got the fan.

6. __ __ can sip a bit __ __ pop.

Unit 4 spellings of high-frequency words, some of which have complex spellings: he, be, me, of. Explain that in the words <he, be, me> the letter <e> has the /ee/ sound and that the letter <f> in the word <of> represents the /v/ sound. Make sure the writer says the sounds as he/she writes the words. This sheet may be photocopied by the purchaser. © Phonic Books Ltd 2013.

Unit 4 - Find the word - Teacher's sheet

he _h_ _e_	be _b_ _e_
me _m_ _e_	of _o_ _f_

Sheet 1

1. "Dan can _be_ the Dad."
2. _He_ can _be_ the Dad.
3. "Get _me_ a map, Viv."
4. "Tam can _be_ a vet."
5. Tam fed Bob a bit _of_ cod.
6. Bob, the cat is sad. _He_ can not fit as _he_ is fat.

Sheet 2

1. "Tam can _be_ the Mum."
2. Get _me_ a peg, Ted.
3. Dan fed Bob a pot _of_ cod.
4. "Pip, get _me_ the fan on the bed."
5. _He_ got the fan.
6. _He_ can sip a bit _of_ pop.

Unit 4 spellings of high-frequency words, some of which have complex spellings: he, be, me, of Explain that in the words <he, be, me> the letter <e> has the /ee/ sound and that the letter <f> in the word <of> represents the /v/ sound. Make sure the writer says the sounds as he/she writes the words. This sheet may be photocopied by the purchaser. © Phonic Books Ltd 2013

Lesson 4
Stepping Stones game

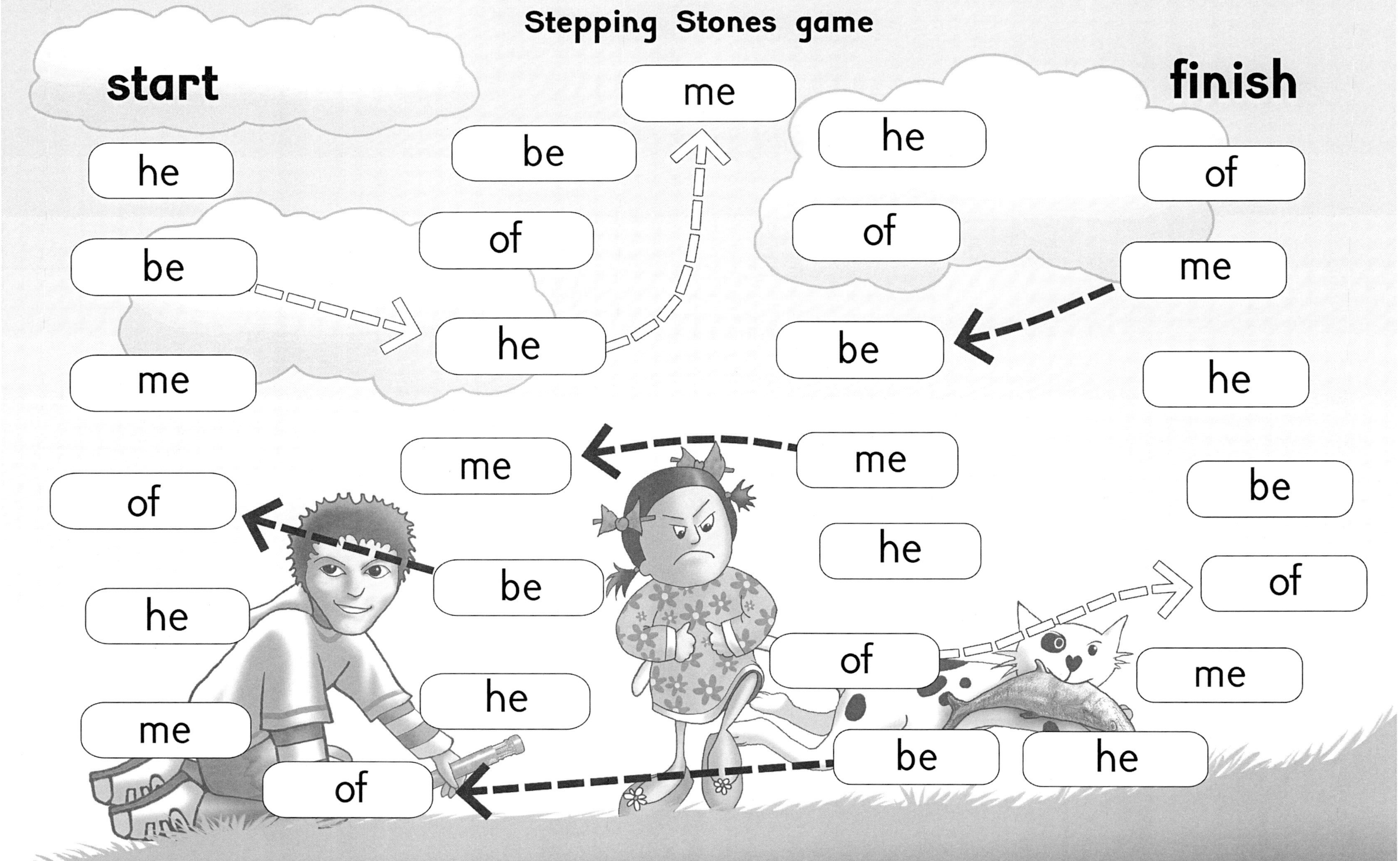

start

he → be → me → of → he → me → be → he → of

me ← he ← of ← be

he → of → be → me → he → of → be

me → of → he → be → of → me

finish

This game is for 1–4 players. Play with counters and die. This sheet may be photocopied by the purchaser. © Phonic Books Ltd. 2013.

4-in-a-Row Game - Unit 4

his	has	he	the	me
be	of	his	be	his
he	has	me	has	of
I	of	his	the	he
be	has	me	is	be
me	he	of	his	me

Two different sets of coloured counters are needed. Two players take it in turns to read the word and put a counter on the word. The winner is the first to get four counters in a row. Play four games. When a game is won, the winner places a counter on the picture at the bottom of the page. This sheet may be photocopied by the purchaser. © Phonic Books Ltd 2013.

Lesson 5 – Unit 5

for

to

put

but

Unit 5 - Find the word (1)

| for __ __ | to __ __ |
| put __ __ __ | but __ __ __ |

1. Pip got a cup __ __ Kim.

2. Ken __ __ __ his bun in the hut.

3. "I can get __ __ the bus if I run."

4. Viv can run __ __ __ can not get to the bus.

5. Pip got Pam in __ __ bed.

6. Kim got gum __ __ Pip.

Unit 5 spellings of high-frequency words, some of which have complex spellings: for, to, put, but. Explain that the sound 'or' in the word <for> has two letters, the letter <o> in <to> represents the sound /oo/ as in <boot> and the letter <u> in the word <put> represents the sound /oo/ as in <look>. Make sure the writer says the sounds as he/she writes the words. This sheet may be photocopied by the purchaser. © Phonic Books Ltd 2013.

Unit 5 - Find the word (2)

| for __ ____ | to __ __ |
| put __ __ __ | but __ __ __ |

1. Bob did not __ __ __ the cod in the bin.

2. Bob got cod __ __ __ Meg did not.

3. Dan had cod __ ____ Bob.

4. Pip __ __ __ Pam in to bed.

5. Pip ran __ __ get a can of pop.

6. Tam is on the bus __ __ __ the bag is not.

Unit 5 spellings of high-frequency words, some of which have complex spellings: for, to, put, but. Explain that the sound 'or' in the word <for> has two letters, the letter <o> in <to> represents the sound /oo/ as in <boot> and the letter <u> in the word <put> represents the sound /oo/ as in <look>. Make sure the writer says the sounds as he/she writes the words. This sheet may be photocopied by the purchaser. © Phonic Books Ltd 2013.

36 Unit 5 - Find the word - Teacher's sheet

for	<u>f</u> <u>or</u>	to	<u>t</u> <u>o</u>
put	<u>p</u> <u>u</u> <u>t</u>	but	<u>b</u> <u>u</u> <u>t</u>

Sheet 1

1. Pip got a cup *for* Kim.
2. Ken *put* his bun in the hut.
3. "I can get *to* the bus if I run."
4. Viv can run *but* can not get to the bus.
5. Pip got Pam in *to* bed.
6. Kim got gum *for* Pip.

Sheet 2

1. Bob did not *put* the cod in the bin.
2. Bob got cod *but* Meg did not.
3. Dan had cod *for* Bob.
4. Pip *put* Pam in to bed.
5. Pip ran *to* get a can of pop.
6. Tam is on the bus *but* the bag is not.

Unit 5 spellings of high-frequency words, some of which have complex spellings: for, to, put, but. Explain that the sound 'or' in the word ‹for› has two letters, the letter ‹o› in ‹to› represents the sound /oo/ as in ‹boot› and the letter ‹u› in the word ‹put› represents the sound /oo/ as in ‹look›. Make sure the writer says the sounds as he/she writes the words. This sheet may be photocopied by the purchaser. © Phonic Books Ltd 2013.

Lesson 5
Stepping Stones game

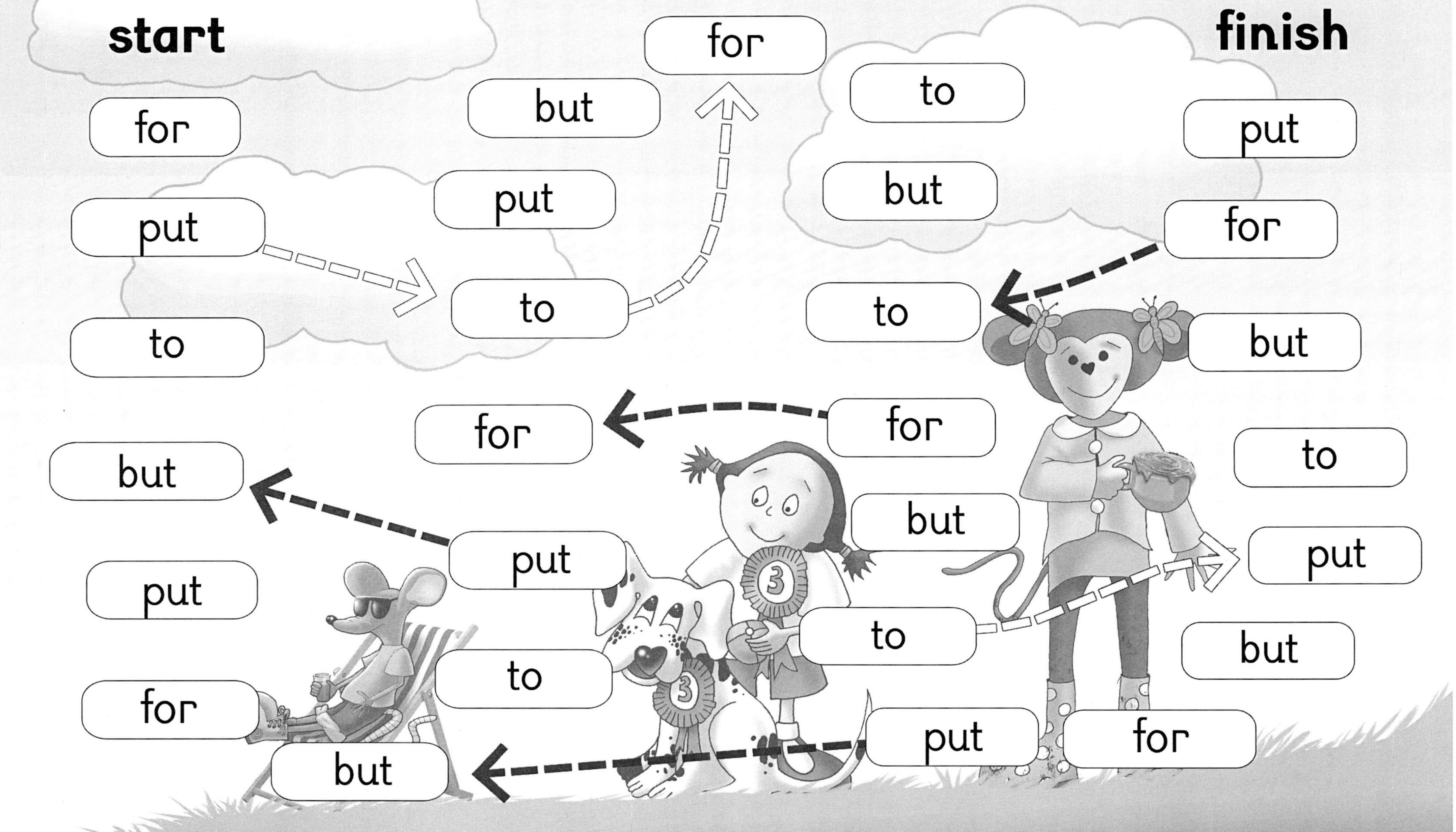

start — for — put — to — but — put — for

for — to — put — but

but — put — to — for — but — to — put — but

to — but — for — to — put

for — but — to — put — for — **finish**

This game is for 1–4 players. Play with counters and die. This sheet may be photocopied by the purchaser. © Phonic Books Ltd. 2013.

4-in-a-Row Game – Unit 5

for	to	he	put	but
be	of	his	for	to
put	has	but	put	of
for	of	for	the	for
be	has	me	put	be
but	he	to	but	I

Two different sets of coloured counters are needed. Two players take it in turns to read the word and put a counter on the word. The winner is the first to get four counters in a row. Play four games. When a game is won, the winner places a counter on the picture at the bottom of the page. This sheet may be photocopied by the purchaser. © Phonic Books Ltd 2013.

Lesson 6 – Unit 6

have

put

was

for

Unit 6 - Find the word (1)

have __ __ ___	put __ __ __
was __ __ __	for __ ___

1. Jim __ __ __ in his big web.

2. Jim can __ __ ___ a bit of jam.

3. Liz __ __ __ the red top on Zig.

4. Zig and Zog __ __ ___ a jet.

5. Liz got a zip __ ___ the red top.

6. Zig and Zog __ __ ___ a bun.

Unit 6 spellings of high-frequency words, some of which have complex spellings: have, put, was, for. Explain that the sound 'or' in the word <for> is represented by two letters, the letter <u> in the word <put> represents the sound /oo/ as in <look>, the letter <a> in <was> represents the sound /o/ and the sound /v/ in <have> is represented by the two letters <ve>. Make sure the writer says the sounds as he/she writes the words. This sheet may be photocopied by the purchaser. © Phonic Books Ltd 2013.

Unit 6 - Find the Word (2)   41

| have __ __ ___ | put __ __ __ |
| was __ __ __ | for __ ___ |

1. Zig and Zog __ __ ___   __ __ __ the bun in the bin __ ___ Meg.

2. The bun __ __ __ not in the wet pit.

3. Ken ran __ ___ his mac.

4. Ken __ __ __ his mac on.

5. Viv __ __ __ sad not to win.

Unit 6 spellings of high-frequency words, some of which have complex spellings: have, put, was, for. Explain that the sound 'or' in the word <for> is represented by two letters, the letter <u> in the word <put> represents the sound /oo/ as in <look>, the letter <a> in <was> represents the sound /o/ and the sound /v/ in <have> is represented by the two letters <ve>. Make sure the writer says the sounds as he/she writes the words. This sheet may be photocopied by the purchaser. © Phonic Books Ltd 2013.

42   Unit 6 - Find the word - Teacher's sheet

have <u>h</u> <u>a</u> <u>ve</u>	put <u>p</u> <u>u</u> <u>t</u>
was <u>w</u> <u>a</u> <u>s</u>	for <u>f</u> <u>or</u>

Sheet 1

1. Jim <u>was</u> in his big web.
2. Jim can <u>have</u> a bit of jam.
3. Liz <u>put</u> the red top on Zig.
4. Zig and Zog <u>have</u> a jet.
5. Liz got a zip <u>for</u> the red top.
6. Zig and Zog <u>have</u> a bun.

Sheet 2

1. Zig and Zog <u>have</u> <u>put</u> the bun in the bin <u>for</u> Meg.
2. The bun <u>was</u> not in the wet pit.
3. Ken ran <u>for</u> his mac.
4. Ken <u>put</u> his mac on.
5. Viv <u>was</u> sad not to win.

Unit 6 spellings of high-frequency words, some of which have complex spellings: have, put, was, for. Explain that the sound 'or' in the word <for> is represented by two letters, the letter <u> in the word <put> represents the sound /oo/ as in <look>, the letter <a> in <was> represents the sound /o/ and the sound /v/ in <have> is represented by the two letters <ve>. Make sure the writer says the sounds as he/she writes the words. This sheet may be photocopied by the purchaser. © Phonic Books Ltd 2013.

Lesson 6
Stepping Stones game

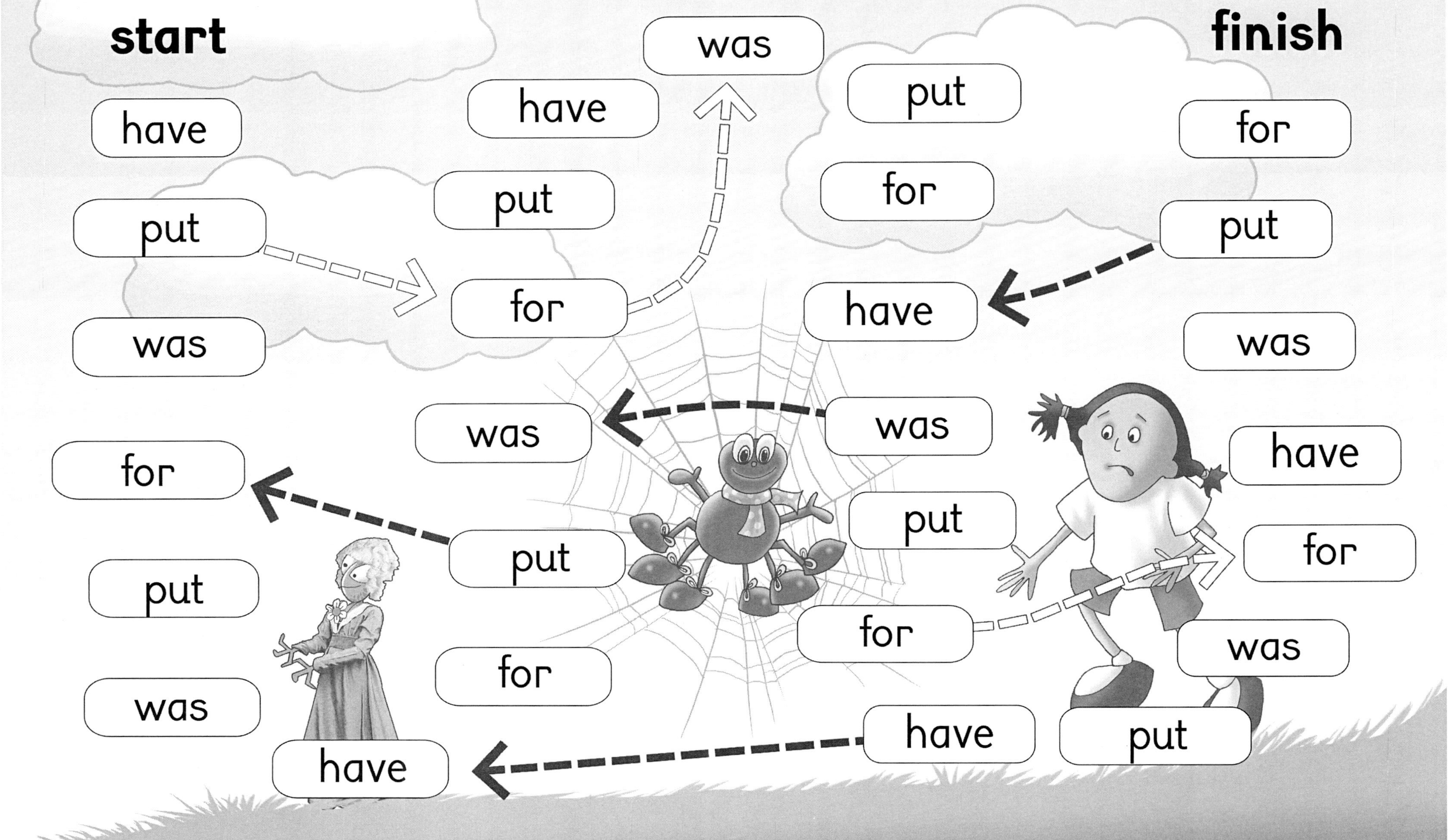

start — have, put, was, for, put, was, have, put, for

have, put, for, was, have, was, put, for, have

put, was, for, put, for, have — **finish**

This game is for 1–4 players. Play with counters and die. This sheet may be photocopied by the purchaser. © Phonic Books Ltd. 2013.

4-in-a-Row Game - Unit 6

for	have	he	put	was
be	of	was	for	to
put	has	have	put	of
for	of	for	was	for
have	has	was	me	be
was	he	put	but	have

Two different sets of coloured counters are needed. Two players take it in turns to read the word and put a counter on the word. The winner is the first to get four counters in a row. Play four games. When a game is won, the winner places a counter on the picture at the bottom of the page. This sheet may be photocopied by the purchaser. © Phonic Books Ltd 2013.

Lesson 7 – Unit 7

you

was

said

off

Unit 7 - Find the word (1)

you __ __	was __ __ __
said __ __ __	off __ __

1. "I will let Bob in," __ __ __ Jill.

2. "__ __ must get __ __ the sill," __ __ __ Jill to Bob.

3. Jill, the doll, __ __ __ in a box.

4. Zog __ __ __ to Jill, "I will get __ __ from the box."

5. Jill __ __ __ on the jet but fell __ __.

Unit 7 spellings of high-frequency words, some of which have complex spellings: you, was, said, off. Explain that the sound of the letters <ou> in the word <you> have the sound /oo/ as in <look>, the sound of the letter <a> in the word <was> is /o/ and the sound of the letters <ai> in the word <said> is /e/. Make sure the writer says the sounds as he/she writes the words. This sheet may be photocopied by the purchaser. © Phonic Books Ltd 2013.

Unit 7 - Find the word (2)

you	__ ___	was	__ __ __
said	__ ___ __	off	__ ___

1. Zig __ ___ __, "Jill, I will fix the leg."

2. Dan and Liz __ ___ __ Bob __ __ __ ill.

3. "I will put __ ___ in a box," __ ___ __ Dan to Bob.

4. Bob ran __ ___ and the rug fell __ ___.

5. Rex __ __ __ sad. He had not got a pal.

Unit 7 spellings of high-frequency words, some of which have complex spellings: you, was, said, off. Explain that the sound of the letters ‹ou› in the word ‹you› have the sound /oo/ as in ‹look›, the sound of the letter ‹a› in the word ‹was› is /o/ and the sound of the letters ‹ai› in the word ‹said› is /e/. Make sure the writer says the sounds as he/she writes the words. This sheet may be photocopied by the purchaser. © Phonic Books Ltd 2013.

Unit 7 - Find the word - Teacher's sheet

you	y ou	was	w a s
said	s ai d	off	o ff

Sheet 1

1. "I will let Bob in," said Jill.

2. "You must get off the sill," said Jill to Bob.

3. Jill, the doll, was in a box.

4. Zog said to Jill, "I will get you from the box."

5. Jill was on the jet but fell off.

Sheet 2

1. Zig said, "Jill, I will fix the leg."

2. Dan and Liz said Bob was ill.

3. "I will put you in a box," said Dan to Bob.

4. Bob ran off and the rug fell off.

5. Rex was sad. He had not got a pal.

Unit 7 spellings of high-frequency words, some of which have complex spellings: you, was, said, off. Explain that the sound of the letters ‹ou› in the word ‹you› have the sound /oo/ as in ‹look›, the sound of the letter ‹a› in the word ‹was› is /o/ and the sound of the letters ‹ai› in the word ‹said› is /e/. Make sure the writer says the sounds as he/she writes the words. This sheet may be photocopied by the purchaser. © Phonic Books Ltd 2013.

Lesson 7
Stepping Stones game

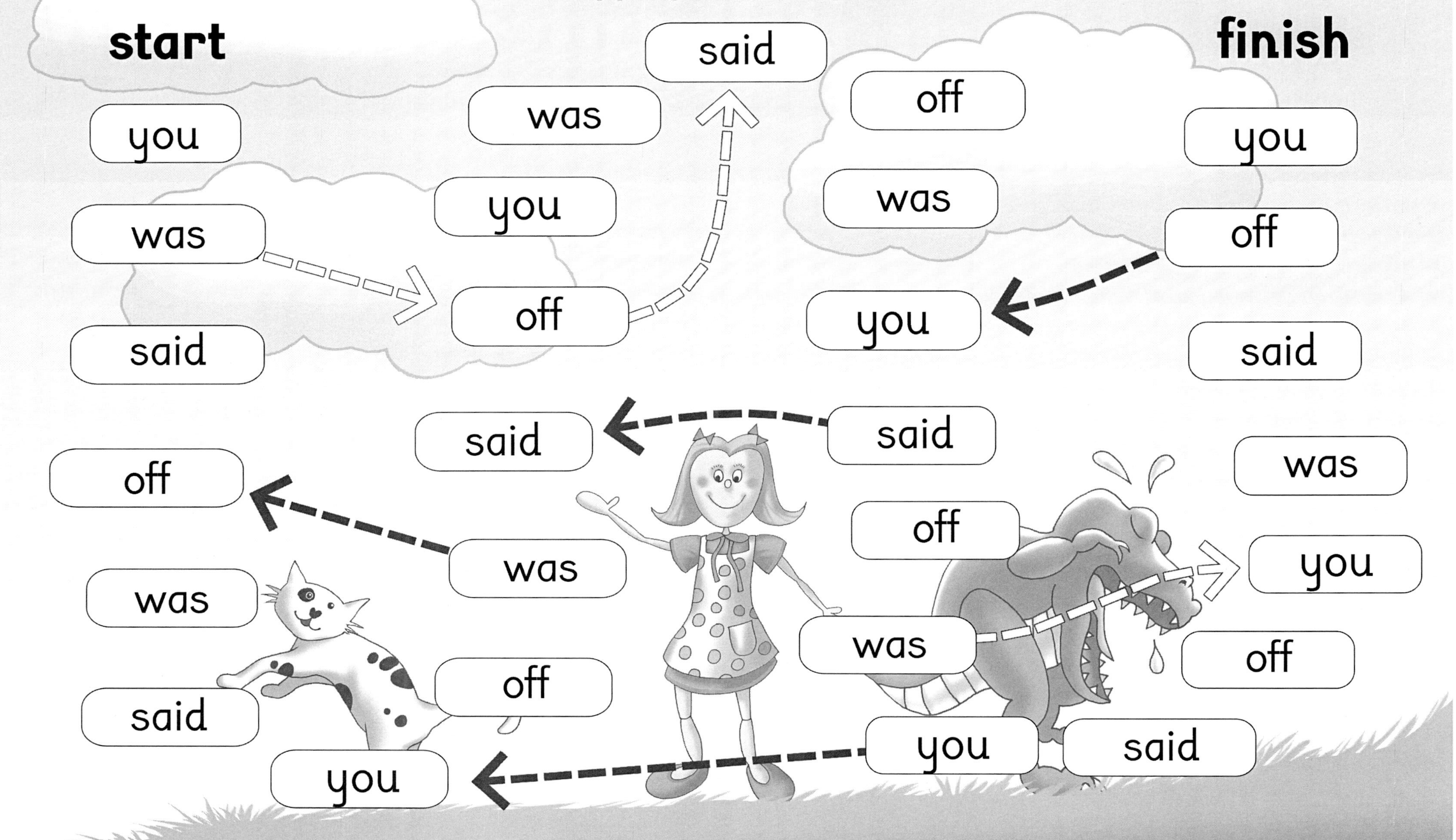

start

finish

you, was, said, off, was, you, said, off, was, said, off, was, you, said, you, off, said, was, you, off, was, said, you, off, said, was, you

This game is for 1–4 players. Play with counters and die. This sheet may be photocopied by the purchaser. © Phonic Books Ltd. 2013.

4-in-a-Row Game - Unit 7

for	you	said	put	was
be	of	was	off	said
put	said	you	put	off
off	of	for	said	you
said	you	was	me	be
was	he	put	you	have

Two different sets of coloured counters are needed. Two players take it in turns to read the word and put a counter on the word. The winner is the first to get four counters in a row. Play four games. When a game is won, the winner places a counter on the picture at the bottom of the page. This sheet may be photocopied by the purchaser. Phonic Books Ltd 2013.

Lesson 8 – Unit 8

don't

say

puts

and

Unit 8 - Find the word (1)

| don't __ __ __'__ | say __ __ __ |
| puts __ __ __ __ | and __ __ __ |

1. Alf __ __ __ __ the tent in the dump.

2. "__ __ __'__ put the tent in the dump," says Hank, "I can mend it."

3. Hank __ __ __ __ up the tent __ __ __ Alf __ __ __ __ the lamp on.

4. Bob __ __ __ Meg jump on to the bunk bed.

5. "__ __ __'__ be sad, Wilf," __ __ __ Liz __ __ __ Viv.

Unit 8 spellings of high-frequency words, some of which have complex spellings: don't, say, puts, and. Explain that the sound of the letter <o> in the word <don't> is /oe/, the sound of the letters <ay> in the word <say> is /ae/ and the sound of the letter <u> in the word <puts> is /oo/ as in <look>. Make sure the writer says the sounds as he/she writes the words. This sheet may be photocopied by the purchaser. © Phonic Books 2013.

Unit 8 - Find the word (2)   53

| don't __ __ __' __ | say __ ____ |
| puts __ __ __ __ | and __ __ __ |

1. Wilf __ __ __ __ elf dust on the leg of the bed.

2. Liz __ __ __ Viv __ ____ Wilf is the best elf.

3. Dad __ __ __ __ a gift in to Alf's hands.

4. Pip and Tess __ __ __, "We must find the lost box."

5. Tess says, "Pip, __ __ __' __ tilt the logs!"

Unit 8 spellings of high-frequency words, some of which have complex spellings: don't, say, puts, and. Explain that the sound of the letter <o> in the word <don't> is /oe/, the sound of the letters <ay> in the word <say> is /ae/ and the sound of the letter <u> in the word <puts> is /oo/ as in <look>. Make sure the writer says the sounds as he/she writes the words. This sheet may be photocopied by the purchaser. © Phonic Books 2013.

Unit 8 - Find the word - Teacher's sheet

don't _d o n' t_	say _s ay_
puts _p u t s_	and _a n d_

Sheet 1

1. Alf _puts_ the tent in the dump.

2. "_Don't_ put the tent in the dump," says Hank, "I can mend it."

3. Hank _puts_ up the tent _and_ Alf _puts_ the lamp on.

4. Bob _and_ Meg jump on to the bunk bed.

5. "_Don't_ be sad, Wilf," _say_ Liz _and_ Viv.

Sheet 2

1. Wilf _puts_ elf dust on the leg of the bed.

2. Liz _and_ Viv _say_ Wilf is the best elf.

3. Dad _puts_ a gift in to Alf's hands.

4. Pip and Tess _say,_ "We must find the lost box."

5. Tess says, "Pip, _don't_ tilt the logs!"

Unit 8 spellings of high-frequency words, some of which have complex spellings: don't, say, puts, and. Explain that the sound of the letter <o> in the word <don't> is /oe/, the sound of the letters <ay> in the word <say> is /ae/ and the sound of the letter <u> in the word <puts> is /oo/ as in <look>. Make sure the writer says the sounds as he/she writes the words. This sheet may be photocopied by the purchaser. © Phonic Books 2013.

Lesson 8
Stepping Stones game

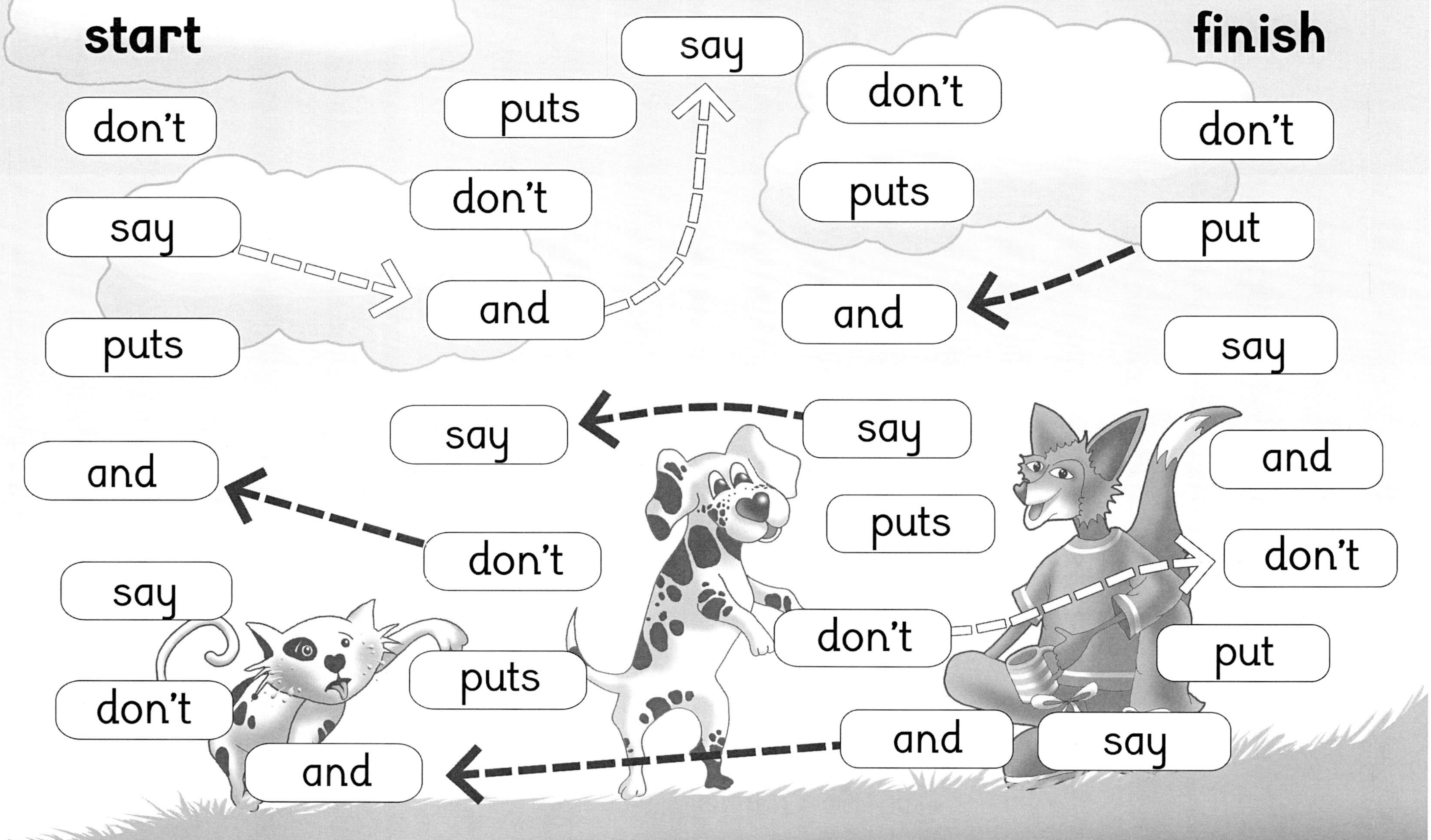

start

finish

don't, say, puts, puts, don't, and, say, puts, don't, put, don't

say, and, say, puts, don't, and, say, and, don't, put, say

and, say, don't, puts, and, don't

This game is for 1–4 players. Play with counters and die. This sheet may be photocopied by the purchaser. © Phonic Books Ltd. 2013.

4-in-a-Row Game - Lesson 8

for	you	say	don't	was
and	of	was	puts	said
puts	don't	off	put	and
and	puts	for	say	you
said	say	was	puts	don't
don't	and	put	you	have

Two different sets of coloured counters are needed. Two players take it in turns to read the word and put a counter on the word. The winner is the first to get four counters in a row. Play four games. When a game is won, the winner places a counter on the picture at the bottom of the page. This sheet may be photocopied by the purchaser. © Phonic Books Ltd 2013.

Lesson 9 – Unit 9

do

says

from

are

Unit 9 - Find the word (1)

do __ __	says __ ____ __
from __ __ __ __	are _____

1. "Let's grab a plum," __ ____ __ Flip to Flop.

2. Flip and Flop _____ in a trap.

3. Flip and Flop fled __ __ __ __ the trap.

4. "You __ __ fit on the sled, Viv," __ ____ __ Wilf.

5. Dan, Wilf and Viv _____ on the sled.

Unit 9 spellings of high-frequency words, some of which have complex spellings: do, says, from, are. Explain that the sound of the letter <o> in the word <do> is /oo/ as in <boot>, the sound of the letters <ay> in the word <says> is '/ae/ and the word <are> has the sound /ar/. Make sure the writer says the sounds as he/she writes the words. This sheet may be photocopied by the purchaser. © Phonic Books 2013.

Unit 9 - Find the word (2)

| do ___ ___ | says ___ ____ ___ |
| from ___ ___ ___ ___ | are _____ |

1. The sled went ___ ___ ___ ___ flag to flag.

2. "I ___ ___ like milk," ___ ____ ___ Bob.

3. Bob has a hot spud ___ ___ ___ ___ Gran.

4. "___ ___ not spill the milk," ___ ____ ___ Mum.

5. Fred and Viv _____ glad to have milk.

6. Rex got Ted ___ ___ ___ ___ the pram.

Unit 9 spellings of high-frequency words, some of which have complex spellings: do, says, from, are. Explain that the sound of the letter <o> in the word <do> is /oo/ as in <boot>, the sound of the letters <ay> in the word <says> is '/ae/ and the word <are> has the sound /ar/. Make sure the writer says the sounds as he/she writes the words. This sheet may be photocopied by the purchaser. © Phonic Books 2013.

Unit 9 - Find the word - Teacher's sheet

do <u>d o</u>		says <u>s ay s</u>	
from <u>f r o m</u>		are <u>are</u>	

Sheet 1

1. "Let's grab a plum," <u>says</u> Flip to Flop.

2. Flip and Flop <u>are</u> in a trap.

3. Flip and Flop fled <u>from</u> the trap.

4. "You <u>do</u> fit on the sled, Viv," <u>says</u> Wilf.

5. Dan, Wilf and Viv <u>are</u> on the sled.

Sheet 2

1. The sled went <u>from</u> flag to flag.

2. "I <u>do</u> like milk," <u>says</u> Bob.

3. Bob has a hot spud <u>from</u> Gran.

4. "<u>Do</u> not spill the milk," <u>says</u> Mum.

5. Fred and Viv <u>are</u> glad to have milk.

6. Rex got Ted <u>from</u> the pram.

Unit 9 spellings of high-frequency words, some of which have complex spellings: do, says, from, are. Explain that the sound of the letter <o> in the word <do> is /oo/ as in <boot>, the sound of the letters <ay> in the word <says> is '/ae/ and the word <are> has the sound /ar/. Make sure the writer says the sounds as he/she writes the words. This sheet may be photocopied by the purchaser. © Phonic Books 2013.

Lesson 9
Stepping Stones game

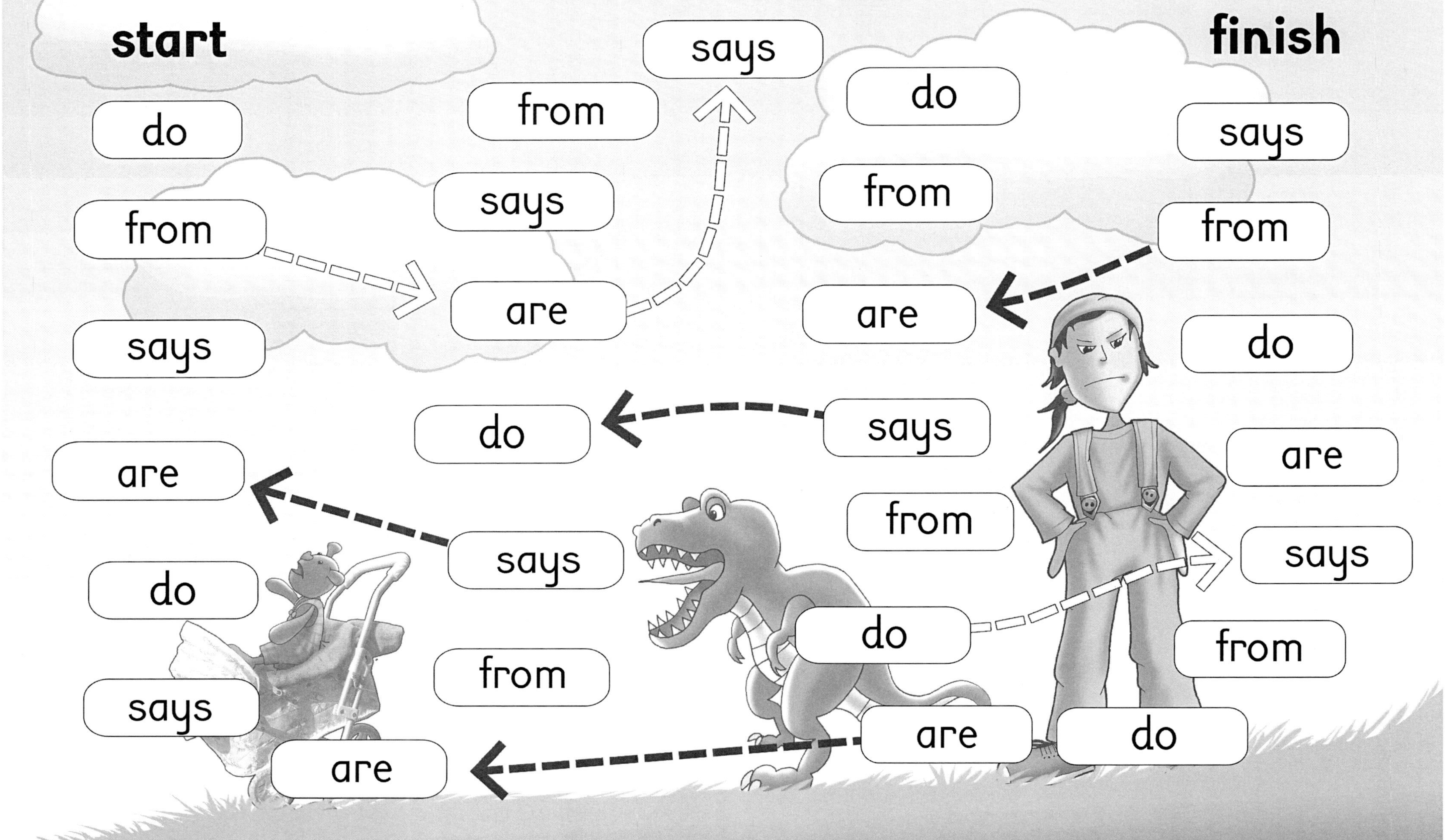

start

finish

do, from, says, are, do, are, says, from, do

from, says, are, do, says, from, do, are

says, from, says, are, says, do, from, are

says, do, are, says, from, do, from, says

This game is for 1–4 players. Play with counters and die. This sheet may be photocopied by the purchaser. © Phonic Books Ltd. 2013.

4-in-a-Row Game - Unit 9

for	do	says	don't	from
from	are	was	puts	said
says	don't	do	are	and
do	are	from	say	says
said	say	was	do	don't
don't	and	are	says	from

Two different sets of coloured counters are needed. Two players take it in turns to read the word and put a counter on the word. The winner is the first to get four counters in a row. Play four games. When a game is won, the winner places a counter on the picture at the bottom of the page. This sheet may be photocopied by the purchaser. © Phonic Books Ltd 2013.

Lesson 10 - Unit 10

don't

says

love

my

Unit 10 - Find the word (1)

| don't __ __ __ ' __ | says __ ____ __ |
| love __ __ ____ | my __ __ |

1. "__ __ __ ' __ let Bob get you, stunt rat."

2. "I __ __ ____ to jump and skip," __ ____ __ Ken.

3. "I __ __ ____ plums. I put __ __ plums in the sand," __ ____ __ Punk.

4. "__ __ __ ' __ scoff bad plums," __ ____ __ Frank to Punk.

Unit 10 spellings of high-frequency words, some of which have complex spellings: don't, says, love, my. Explain that the sound of the letter <o> in the word <don't> represents the sound /oe/, the sound of the letters <ay> in the word <says> represents the sound /ae'/, the letters <ve> in the word <love> represent the sound /v/ and the letter <y> in the word <my> represents the sound /ie/. Make sure the writer says the sounds as he/she writes the words. This sheet may be photocopied by the purchaser. © Phonic Books Ltd 2013.

Unit 10 - Find the word (2)

don't __ __ __'__	says __ ___ __
love __ __ ___	my __ __

1. "I __ __ ___ crisps," __ ___ __ Viv.

2. "I __ __ ___ to swim," __ ___ __ Frank.

3. "I have a gift from __ __ Dad," __ ___ __ Dan.

4. "__ __ __'__ stand on __ __ stilts, Liz," __ ___ __ Dan.

5. "__ __ stilts let me get the egg into the nest," __ ___ __ Dan.

Unit 10 spellings of high-frequency words, some of which have complex spellings: don't, says, love, my. Explain that the sound of the letter <o> in the word <don't> represents the sound /oe/, the sound of the letters <ay> in the word <says> represents the sound /ae'/, the letters <ve> in the word <love> represent the sound /v/ and the letter <y> in the word <my> represents the sound /ie/. Make sure the writer says the sounds as he/she writes the words. This sheet may be photocopied by the purchaser. © Phonic Books Ltd 2013.

Unit 10 - Find the word - Teacher's sheet

| don't <u>d</u> o <u>n't</u> | says <u>s</u> <u>ay</u> <u>s</u> |
| love <u>l</u> o <u>ve</u> | my <u>m</u> <u>y</u> |

Sheet 1

1. "<u>Don't</u> let Bob get you, stunt rat."

2. "I <u>love</u> to jump and skip," <u>says</u> Ken.

3. "I <u>love</u> plums. I put <u>my</u> plums in the sand," <u>says</u> Punk.

4. "<u>Don't</u> scoff bad plums," <u>says</u> Frank to Punk.

Sheet 2

1. "I <u>love</u> crisps," <u>says</u> Viv.

2. "I <u>love</u> to swim," <u>says</u> Frank.

3. "I have a gift from <u>my</u> Dad," <u>says</u> Dan.

4. "<u>Don't</u> stand on <u>my</u> stilts, Liz," <u>says</u> Dan.

5. "<u>My</u> stilts let me get the egg into the nest," <u>says</u> Dan.

Unit 10 spellings of high-frequency words, some of which have complex spellings: don't, says, love, my. Explain that the sound of the letter <o> in the word <don't> represents the sound /oe/, the sound of the letters <ay> in the word <says> represents the sound /ae'/, the letters <ve> in the word <love> represent the sound /v/ and the letter <y> in the word <my> represents the sound /ie/. Make sure the writer says the sounds as he/she writes the words. This sheet may be photocopied by the purchaser. © Phonic Books Ltd 2013.

Lesson 10
Stepping Stones game

start

finish

don't, my, says, love, my, says, love, don't, my, says, love, my, don't, says, love, don't, my, says, love, don't, my, says, love, my, says, don't, my, love

This game is for 1–4 players. Play with counters and die. This sheet may be photocopied by the purchaser. © Phonic Books Ltd. 2013.

4-in-a-Row Game - Unit 10

for	my	says	don't	from
from	are	love	puts	my
says	don't	do	are	love
do	love	my	say	don't
said	say	was	love	my
don't	love	are	says	from

Two different sets of coloured counters are needed. Two players take it in turns to read the word and put a counter on the word. The winner is the first to get four counters in a row. Play four games. When a game is won, the winner places a counter on the picture at the bottom of the page. This sheet may be photocopied by the purchaser. © Phonic Books Ltd 2013.

Lesson 11 – Unit 11

such

we

see

her

Unit 11 - Find the word (1)

such __ __ ____	we __ __
see __ ____	her __ ____

1. Ken and his pals __ ____ a chip in the mud.

2. "__ __ want the chip in the mud," say the kids.

3. Sam and Tam went to bed. Sam got the chess set and put it on __ ____ bed.

4. Dad can __ ____ the chess set on Tam's bed.

5. "Rex has __ __ ____ a big jump!" said Chimp.

Unit 11 spellings of high-frequency words, some of which have complex spellings: such, we, see, her. Explain that the sound of the letter <e> in the word <we> represents the sound /ee/, the letters <ee> in word <see> represent the sound /ee/ and the letters <er> in the word <her> represent the sound /er/. Make sure the writer says the sounds as he/she writes the words. This sheet may be photocopied by the purchaser. © Phonic Books Ltd 2013.

Unit 11 - Find the word (2)

such __ __ ____	we __ __
see __ ____	her __ ____

1. Jill can skip well. Chimp can __ ____ __ ____ skip. "Jill is __ __ ____ a champ!"

2. "__ __ can __ ____ Chimp jump from branch to branch," says Jill. "He is __ __ ____ a champ!"

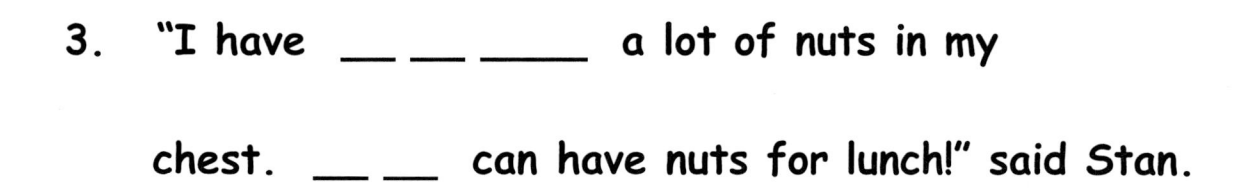

3. "I have __ __ ____ a lot of nuts in my chest. __ __ can have nuts for lunch!" said Stan.

4. Liz is a chess champ. Chen put __ ____ chess set on the grass.

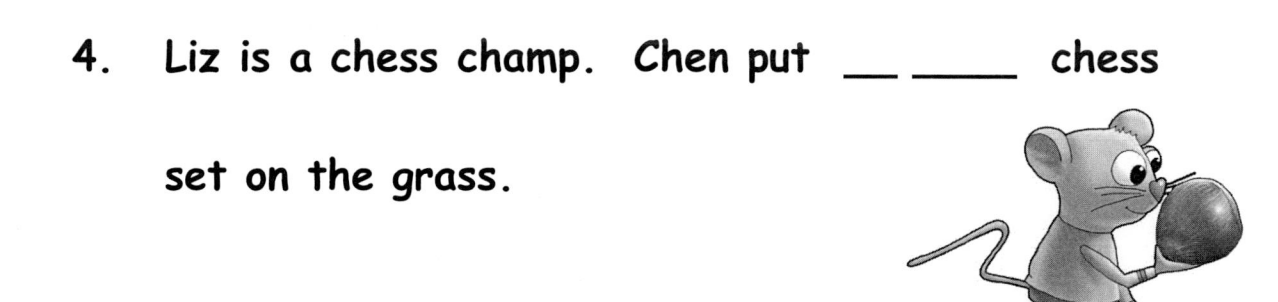

Unit 11 spellings of high-frequency words, some of which have complex spellings: such, we, see, her. Explain that the sound of the letter <e> in the word <we> represents the sound /ee/, the letters <ee> in word <see> represent the sound /ee/ and the letters <er> in the word <her> represent the sound /er/. Make sure the writer says the sounds as he/she writes the words. This sheet may be photocopied by the purchaser. © Phonic Books Ltd 2013.

Unit 11 - Find the word - Teacher's sheet

such <u>s</u> <u>u</u> <u>ch</u>	we <u>w</u> <u>e</u>
see <u>s</u> <u>ee</u>	her <u>h</u> <u>er</u>

Sheet 1

1. Ken and his pals <u>see</u> a chip in the mud.

2. "<u>We</u> want the chip in the mud," say the kids.

3. Sam and Tam went to bed. Sam got the chess set and put it on <u>her</u> bed.

4. Dad can <u>see</u> the chess set on Tam's bed.

5. "Rex has <u>such</u> a big jump!", said Chimp.

Sheet 2

1. Jill can skip well. Chimp can <u>see</u> <u>her</u> skip. "Jill is <u>such</u> a champ!"

2. "<u>We</u> can <u>see</u> Chimp jump from branch to branch," says Jill. "He is <u>such</u> a champ!"

3. "I have <u>such</u> a lot of nuts in my chest. <u>We</u> can have nuts for lunch!" said Stan.

4. Liz is a chess champ. Chen put <u>her</u> chess set on the grass.

Unit 11 spellings of high-frequency words, some of which have complex spellings: such, we, see, her. Explain that the sound of the letter <e> in the word <we> represents the sound /ee/, the letters <ee> in word <see> represent the sound /ee/ and the letters <er> in the word <her> represent the sound /er/. Make sure the writer says the sounds as he/she writes the words. This sheet may be photocopied by the purchaser. © Phonic Books Ltd 2013.

Lesson 11
Stepping Stones game

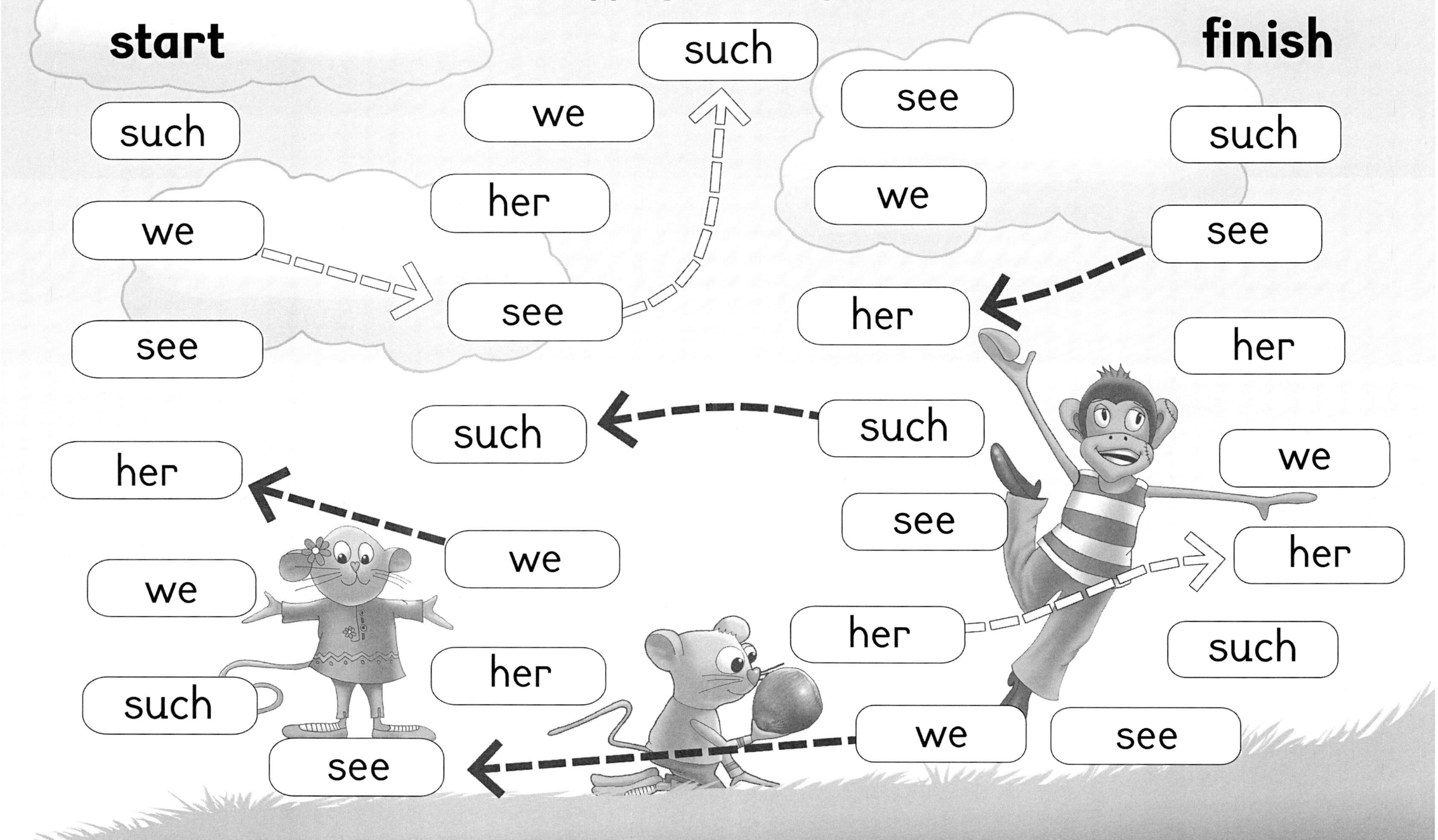

start — **finish**

such, we, see, her, we, such, her, see

we, her, see, such, see, we, her, such

such, we, see, her, we, such, her, see

This game is for 1-4 players. Play with counters and die. This sheet may be photocopied by the purchaser. © Phonic Books Ltd. 2013.

74 4-in-a-Row Game - Unit 11

we	see	says	such	her
her	are	love	see	puts
says	don't	such	we	love
see	my	her	say	don't
said	we	see	love	her
don't	such	are	her	we

Two different sets of coloured counters are needed. Two players take it in turns to read the word and put a counter on the word. The winner is the first to get four counters in a row. Play four games. When a game is won, the winner places a counter on the picture at the bottom of the page. This sheet may be photocopied by the purchaser. © Phonic Books Ltd 2013.

Lesson 12 - Unit 12

she

wish

give

live

Unit 12 - Find the word (1)

| she ____ __ | wish __ __ ____ |
| give __ __ ____ | live __ __ ____ |

1. Bob has a __ __ ____. "I __ __ ____ I had a fish on a dish."

2. The fish __ __ ____ in the pond.

3. Mum asks Josh for the dish. ____ __ gets buns from the shop.

4. "I __ __ ____ I had a pal," said Tosh.

5. "I will __ __ ____ you the ball," says Shep.

Unit 12 spellings of high-frequency words, some of which have complex spellings: she, wish, give, live. Explain that the letter <e> in the word <she> represents the sound /ee/ and the letters <ve> in the words <give, live> represent the sound /v/. Make sure the writer says the sounds as he/she writes the words. This sheet may be photocopied by the purchaser. © Phonic Books Ltd 2013.

Unit 12 - Find the word (2)

| she ____ __ | wish __ __ ____ |
| give __ __ ____ | live __ __ ____ |

1. "Mud on the mat!" says Mum. ____ __ is cross.

2. Flip and Flop __ __ ____ in a tree.

3. "Let us grab Mum for fun!" says Sam. "Help!" ____ __ says.

4. "I __ __ ____ with Dan," said Bob.

5. "I will __ __ ____ you the cash to go to the shop," said Mum.

Unit 12 spellings of high-frequency words, some of which have complex spellings: she, wish, give, live. Explain that the letter <e> in the word <she> represents the sound /ee/ and the letters <ve> in the words <give, live> represent the sound /v/. Make sure the writer says the sounds as he/she writes the words. This sheet may be photocopied by the purchaser. © Phonic Books Ltd 2013.

Unit 12 - Find the word – Teacher's sheet

she	_sh_ _e_	wish	_w_ _i_ _sh_
give	_g_ _i_ _ve_	live	_l_ _i_ _ve_

Sheet 1

1. Bob has a _wish_. "I _wish_ I had a fish on a dish."

2. The fish _live_ in the pond.

3. Mum asks Josh for the dish. _She_ gets buns from the shop.

4. "I _wish_ I had a pal," said Tosh.

5. "I will _give_ you the ball," says Shep.

Sheet 2

1. "Mud on the mat!" says Mum. _She_ is cross.

2. Flip and Flop _live_ in a tree.

3. "Let us grab Mum!" says Sam. "Help!" _she_ says.

4. "I _live_ with Dan," said Bob.

5. "I will _give_ you the cash to go and shop," said Mum.

Unit 12 spellings of high-frequency words, some of which have complex spellings: she, wish, give, live. Explain that the letter <e> in the word <she> represents the sound /ee/ and the letters <ve> in the words <give, live> represent the sound /v/. Make sure the writer says the sounds as he/she writes the words. This sheet may be photocopied by the purchaser. © Phonic Books Ltd 2013.

Lesson 12
Stepping Stones game

start

finish

she — wish — give — live — wish — she — give

give — live — she — wish

she — live — wish

give — wish — she — live

wish — give — she — live — wish — give

This game is for 1–4 players. Play with counters and die. This sheet may be photocopied by the purchaser. © Phonic Books Ltd. 2013.

4-in-a-Row Game - Unit 12

live	see	give	such	her
her	wish	she	see	live
she	live	such	wish	love
see	give	her	give	don't
said	we	love	she	wish
don't	wish	are	her	we

Two different sets of coloured counters are needed. Two players take it in turns to read the word and put a counter on the word. The winner is the first to get four counters in a row. Play four games. When a game is won, the winner places a counter on the picture at the bottom of the page. This sheet may be photocopied by the purchaser. © Phonic Books Ltd 2013.

Lesson 13

this

that

they

with

Unit 13 - Find the word (1)

this ____ __ __	that ____ __ __
they ____ ____	with __ __ ____

1. "Will ____ __ __ fit?" asks Fred. "____ __ __ will not fit," says Mum.

2. "Can I have a bit of ____ __ __ and a bit of ____ __ __?" says Beth.

3. Beth and Frank sat in the camp. ____ ____ drank from a mug __ __ ____ hot broth in it.

4. "____ __ __ thump is a branch ____ __ __ hit the tent," says Frank.

Unit 13 spellings of high-frequency words, some of which have complex spellings: this, that, they, with. Explain that the letters <ey> in the word <they> represent the sound /ae/. Make sure the writer says the sounds as he/she writes the words. This sheet may be photocopied by the purchaser. © Phonic Books Ltd 2013.

Lesson 13 - Find the word (2)

this ___ __ __	that ___ __ __
they ___ ___	with __ __ ___

1. "I can play __ __ ___ a bat and a ball," says Pip.

2. Dad sits at his desk. "___ __ __ will be fun. I can fix the last bit."

3. Sam and Tam rush in and ___ ___ thump the desk. Dad is cross.

4. ___ ___ fix a den for Dad __ __ ___ a desk and a thin mat.

Unit 13 spellings of high-frequency words, some of which have complex spellings: this, that, they, with. Explain that the letters <ey> in the word <they> represent the sound /ae/. Make sure the writer says the sounds as he/she writes the words. This sheet may be photocopied by the purchaser. © Phonic Books Ltd 2013.

Unit 13 - Find the word – Teacher's sheet

| this _th i s_ | that _th a t_ |
| they _th ey_ | with _w i th_ |

Sheet 1

1. "Will _this_ fit?" asks Fred. "_That_ will not fit," says Mum.

2. "Can I have a bit of _this_ and a bit of _that?_" says Beth.

3. Beth and Frank sat in the camp. _They_ drank from a mug _with_ hot broth in it.

4. "_That_ thump is a branch _that_ hit the tent," says Frank.

Sheet 2

1. "I can play _with_ a bat and a ball," says Pip.

2. Dad sits at his desk. "_This_ will be fun. I can fix the last bit."

3. Sam and Tam rush in and _they_ thump the desk. Dad is cross.

4. _They_ fix a den for Dad _with_ a desk and a thin mat.

Unit 13 spellings of high-frequency words, some of which have complex spellings: this, that, they, with. Explain that the letters ‹ey› in the word ‹they› represent the sound /ae/. Make sure the writer says the sounds as he/she writes the words. This sheet may be photocopied by the purchaser. © Phonic Books Ltd 2013.

Lesson 13
Stepping Stones game

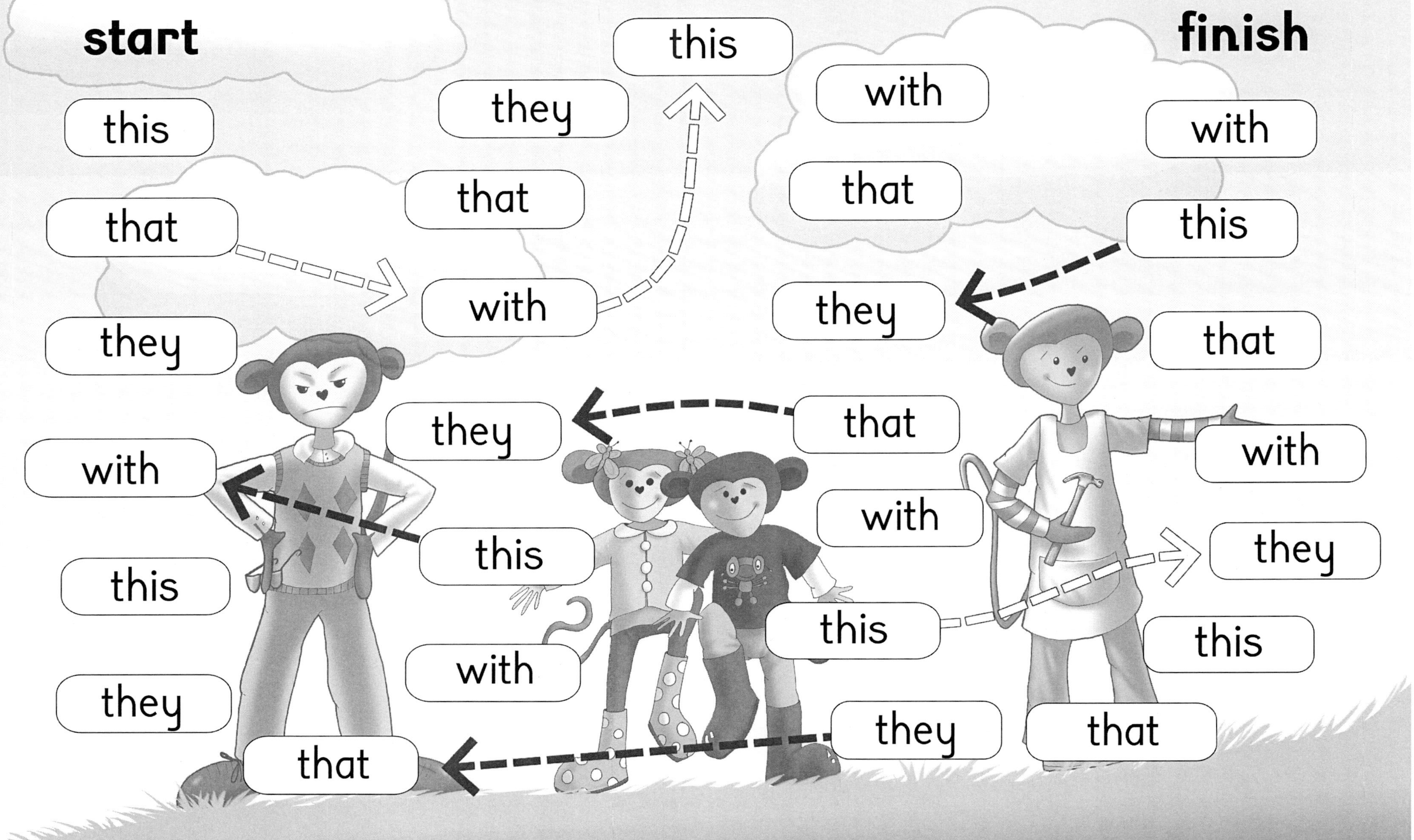

start

finish

this — that — they — with — this — that — they — with — this — that — they — with — this — that — they — with — this — that — they — with — this — that — they — with

This game is for 1–4 players. Play with counters and die. This sheet may be photocopied by the purchaser. © Phonic Books Ltd. 2013.

4-in-a-Row Game - Unit 13

this	see	give	such	they
her	wish	with	this	live
with	live	they	wish	that
see	give	with	give	don't
that	this	love	they	wish
don't	they	are	this	her

Two different sets of coloured counters are needed. Two players take it in turns to read the word and put a counter on the word. The winner is the first to get four counters in a row. Play four games. When a game is won, the winner places a counter on the picture at the bottom of the page. This sheet may be photocopied by the purchaser. © Phonic Books Ltd 2013.

Lesson 14 -Unit 14

no

go

so

old

Unit 14 - Find the word (1)

no __ __	go __ __
so __ __	old __ __ __

1. "Did you pack a snack?" asked Mum. "__ __, I did not," said Viv.

2. Viv got on the __ __ __ bus with __ __ back pack.

3. Jim put his __ __ __ socks in the bin. "I must __ __ to the sock shop," Jim thinks.

4. Josh and Mum __ __ to the sandpit. "It is __ __ much fun in the sand," thinks Josh.

Unit 14 spellings of high frequency words, some of which have complex spellings: no, go, so, old. Explain that the letter <o> in the words <no, go, so, old> represent the sound 'o'. Make sure the writer says the sounds as he/she writes the words. This sheet may be photocopied by the purchaser. © Phonic Books Ltd 2013.

Unit 14 - Find the word (2)

no __ __	go __ __
so __ __	old __ __

1. "Raj, get up," says Mum. "__ __, I am ill," says Raj.

2. Raj put red spots on his neck. It is an __ __ __ trick. "I am ill, Mum," says Raj.

3. At 8 o'clock the kids __ __ to get the bus.

4. "Dad has a clock that is __ __ __ __ __," thinks Raj. "I will __ __ to the shop and get him a clock."

5. "I will get socks as a gift for Mum. Her socks are __ __ __ __ __."

Unit 14 spellings of high frequency words, some of which have complex spellings: no, go, so, old. Explain that the letter <o> in the words <no, go, so, old> represent the sound 'o'. Make sure the writer says the sounds as he/she writes the words. This sheet may be photocopied by the purchaser. © Phonic Books Ltd 2013.

Unit 14 - Find the word - Teacher's sheet

no	<u>n</u> <u>o</u>	go	<u>g</u> <u>o</u>
so	<u>s</u> <u>o</u>	old	<u>o</u> <u>l</u> <u>d</u>

Sheet 1

1. "Did you pack a snack?" asked Mum. "<u>No</u>, I did not," said Viv.

2. Viv got on the <u>old</u> bus with <u>no</u> back pack.

3. Jim put his <u>old</u> socks in the bin. "I must <u>go</u> to the sock shop," Jim thinks.

4. Josh and Mum <u>go</u> to the sandpit. "It is <u>so</u> much fun in the sand," thinks Josh.

Sheet 2

1. "Raj, get up," says Mum. "<u>No</u>, I am ill," says Raj.

2. Raj put red spots on his neck. It is an <u>old</u> trick. "I am ill, Mum," says Raj.

3. At 8 o'clock, the kids <u>go</u> to get the bus.

4. "Dad has a clock that is <u>so</u> <u>old</u>," thinks Raj. "I will <u>go</u> to the shop and get him a clock."

5. "I will get socks as a gift for Mum. Her socks are <u>so</u> <u>old</u>."

Unit 14 spellings of high frequency words, some of which have complex spellings: no, go, so, old. Explain that the letter <o> in the words <no, go, so, old> represent the sound 'o'. Make sure the writer says the sounds as he/she writes the words. This sheet may be photocopied by the purchaser. © Phonic Books Ltd 2013.

Lesson 14
Stepping Stones game

start

finish

no – go – so – old – go – so
old – go – so – old – no
no – go – old
old – go – so – no
old – so – go – no – old
go – so – go – no – old – go

This game is for 1–4 players. Play with counters and die. This sheet may be photocopied by the purchaser. © Phonic Books Ltd. 2013.

4-in-a-Row Game - Unit 14

this	see	no	such	they
her	wish	old	this	live
with	go	they	so	that
no	old	with	go	don't
that	this	love	they	old
go	they	old	this	her

Two different sets of coloured counters are needed. Two players take it in turns to read the word and put a counter on the word. The winner is the first to get four counters in a row. Play four games. When a game is won, the winner places a counter on the picture at the bottom of the page. This sheet may be photocopied by the purchaser. © Phonic Books Ltd 2013.

Lesson 15 - Unit 15

long

along

going

think

Unit 15 - Find the word (1)

long __ __ ___	along __ __ __ ___
going __ __ __ ___	think ___ __ __ __

1. Dot ran __ __ __ ___ a stem and sang a song.

2. Dot felt a strong wind and clung to the __ __ ___ stem.

3. "Help! I am __ __ __ ___ to end up in the pond," said Dot.

4. "Dot, grab the __ __ ___ bit of string!" yells Pip.

5. "I ___ __ __ __ it is spring," said Red Bill. "Let us all sing a __ __ ___ spring song."

Unit 15 spellings of high-frequency words, some of which have complex spellings: long, along, going, think. Explain that the letter <o> in the word <going> represents the sound 'o'. Point out that <going, along> are two syllable words. Make sure the writer says the sounds as he/she writes the words. This sheet may be photocopied by the purchaser. © Phonic Books Ltd 2013.

Unit 15 - Find the word (2)   95

| long __ __ ___ | along __ __ __ ___ |
| going __ __ __ ___ | think ___ __ __ __ |

1. "Stop that song," said Sam. But then he said," I ___ __ __ __ I am __ __ __ ___ to sing __ __ __ ___ with them."

2. Ken, the rat, fixes a bell on to the dog. "I do not ___ __ __ __ he is __ __ __ ___ to get me. if the bell rings I will run __ __ __ ___ the __ __ ___ path."

3. Flip and Flop cling to a __ __ ___ branch. Flip tells Flop to get the thing that glints in the grass Flop says, "I am __ __ __ ___ to get it," and flaps his wings.

Unit 15 spellings of high-frequency words, some of which have complex spellings: long, along, going, think. Explain that the letter <o> in the word <going> represents the sound 'o'. Point out that <going, along> are two syllable words. Make sure the writer says the sounds as he/she writes the words. This sheet may be photocopied by the purchaser. © Phonic Books Ltd 2013.

Unit 15 - Find the word – Teacher's sheet

| long _l_ _o_ _ng_ | along _a_ _l_ _o_ _ng_ |
| going _g_ _o_ _i_ _ng_ | think _th_ _i_ _n_ _k_ |

Sheet 1

1. Dot ran _along_ a stem and sang a song.

2. Dot felt a strong wind and clung to the _long_ stem.

3. "Help! I am _going_ to end up in the pond," said Dot.

4. "Dot, grab the _long_ bit of string!" yells Pip.

5. "I _think_ it is spring," said Red Bill. "Let us all sing a _long_ spring song."

Sheet 2

1. "Stop that song," said Sam. But then he said," I _think_ I am _going_ to sing _along_ with them."

2. Ken, the rat, fixes a bell onto the dog. "I do not _think_ he is _going_ to get me. If the bell rings I will run _along_ the _long_ path."

3. Flip and Flop cling to a _long_ branch. Flip tells Flop to get the thing that glints in the grass. Flop says, "I am _going_ to get it," and flaps his wings.

Unit 15 spellings of high-frequency words, some of which have complex spellings: long, along, going, think. Explain that the letter <o> in the word <going> represents the sound 'o'. Point out that <going, along> are two syllable words. Make sure the writer says the sounds as he/she writes the words. This sheet may be photocopied by the purchaser. © Phonic Books Ltd 2013.

Lesson 15
Stepping Stones game

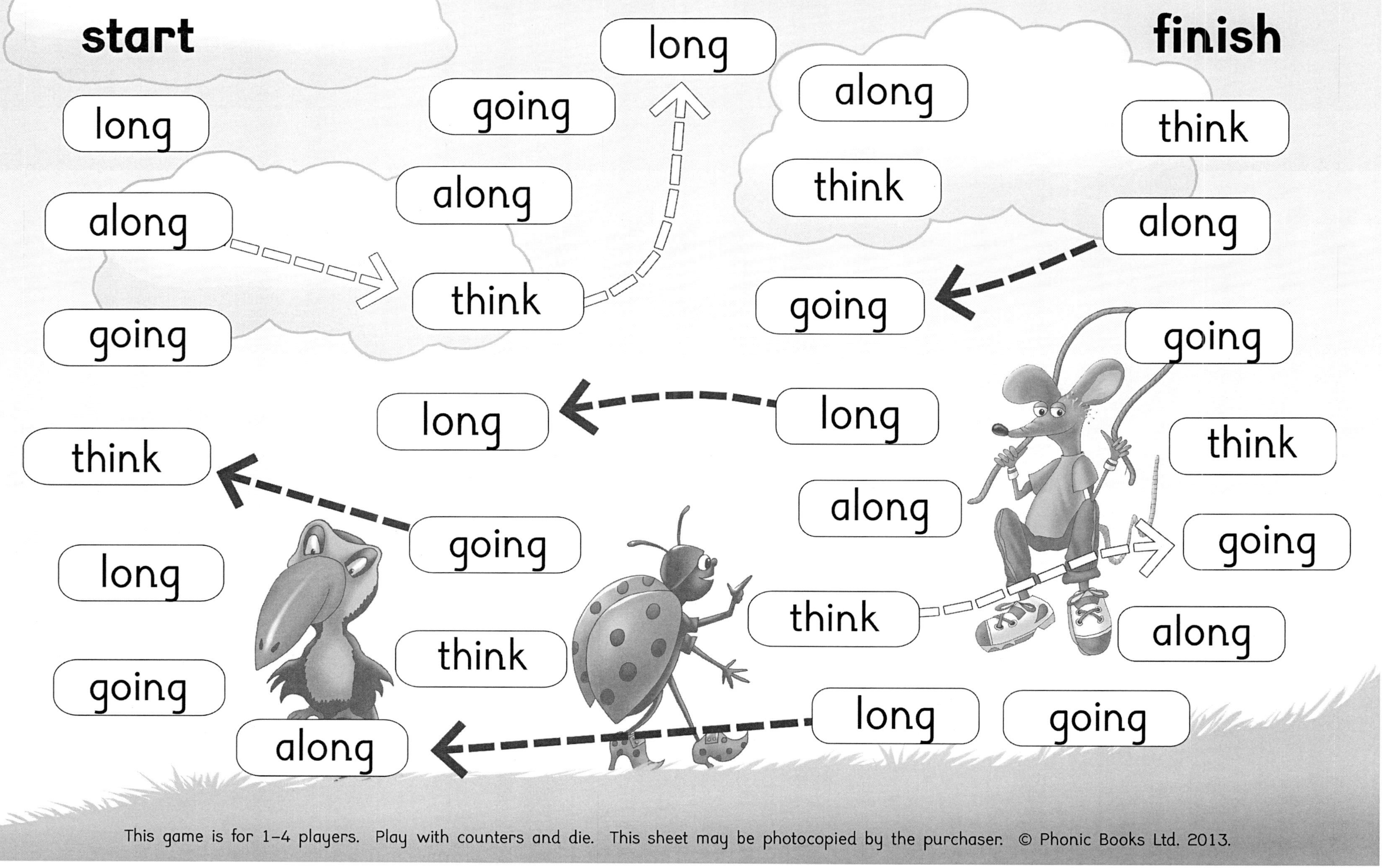

start → long, along, going, think, long, going, along, think, along, going, think, long, going, along, think, long, going, along, think, going, **finish**

This game is for 1–4 players. Play with counters and die. This sheet may be photocopied by the purchaser. © Phonic Books Ltd. 2013.

4-in-a-Row Game - Unit 15

this	long	no	along	they
her	think	old	this	live
they	go	going	so	long
think	along	with	long	think
that	going	think	they	old
go	they	long	this	going

Two different sets of coloured counters are needed. Two players take it in turns to read the word and put a counter on the word. The winner is the first to get four counters in a row. Play four games. When a game is won, the winner places a counter on the picture at the bottom of the page. This sheet may be photocopied by the purchaser. © Phonic Books Ltd 2013.

Lesson 16 - Unit 16

loves

have

lives

gives

Unit 16 - Find the word (1)

love(s) __ __ ___ (__)   have __ __ ___

live(s) __ __ ___ (__)   give(s) __ __ ___ (__)

1. The squid __ __ ___ __ on the rocks. He says, "I can help with the chest. I __ __ ___ lots of hands."

2. The squid __ __ ___ __ to __ __ ___ the rings Tess __ __ ___ __ him.

3. Quin __ __ ___ __ with Chen. Chen __ __ ___ __ Quin. He lets Quin get into bed with him.

4. Mum says, "I will not __ __ ___ a dog in a bed! I will __ __ ___ Quin back to the pet shop!"

Unit 16 spellings of high-frequency words, some of which have complex spellings: love(s), live(s), give(s), have. Explain that the letter <o> in the word < love > represents the 'u' sound. Make sure the writer says the sounds as he/she writes the words. This sheet may be photocopied by the purchaser. © Phonic Books Ltd 2013.

Unit 16 - Find the word (2)   101

| love(s) | __ __ ____ (__) | have | __ __ ____ |
| live(s) | __ __ ____ (__) | give(s) | __ __ ____ (__) |

1. "No, Mum, no!" says Chen. "I __ __ ____ Quin! You must not __ __ ____ him back!"

2. "I will make Quin a quilt." Dan and Liz __ __ ____ Chen bits of cloth.

3. Chen says, "I __ __ ____ cloth but cannot fix a quilt." Nan can. Nan __ __ ____ __ the quilt to Quin the pup.

4. Quin __ __ ____ __ his quilt. He is as snug as a bug in a rug and will not go to the shop with Chen.

Unit 16 spellings of high-frequency words, some of which have complex spellings: love(s), live(s), give(s), have. Explain that the letter <o> in the word < love > represents the 'u' sound. Make sure the writer says the sounds as he/she writes the words. This sheet may be photocopied by the purchaser. © Phonic Books Ltd 2013.

Unit 16 - Find the word – Teacher's sheet

> love l *o* ve (s)   have h *a* ve
>
> live l *i* ve (s)   give g *i* ve (s)

Sheet 1

1. The squid *lives* on the rocks. He says, "I can help with the chest. I *have* lots of hands."

2. The squid *loves* to *have* the rings Tess *gives* him.

3. Quin *lives* with Chen. Chen *loves* Quin. He lets Quin get in to bed with him.

4. Mum says, "I will not *have* a dog in a bed! I will *give* Quin back to the pet shop!"

Sheet 2

1. "No, Mum, no!" says Chen. "I *love* Quin! You must not *give* him back!"

2. "I will make Quin a quilt." Dan and Liz *give* Chen bits of cloth.

3. Chen says, "I *have* cloth but cannot fix a quilt." Nan can. Nan *gives* the quilt to Quin, the pup.

4. Quin *loves* his quilt. He is as snug as a bug in a rug and will not go to the shop with Chen.

Unit 16 spellings of high-frequency words, some of which have complex spellings: love(s), live(s), give(s), have. Explain that the letter <o> in the word < love > represents the 'u' sound. Make sure the writer says the sounds as he/she writes the words. This sheet may be photocopied by the purchaser. © Phonic Books Ltd 2013.

Lesson 16
Stepping Stones game

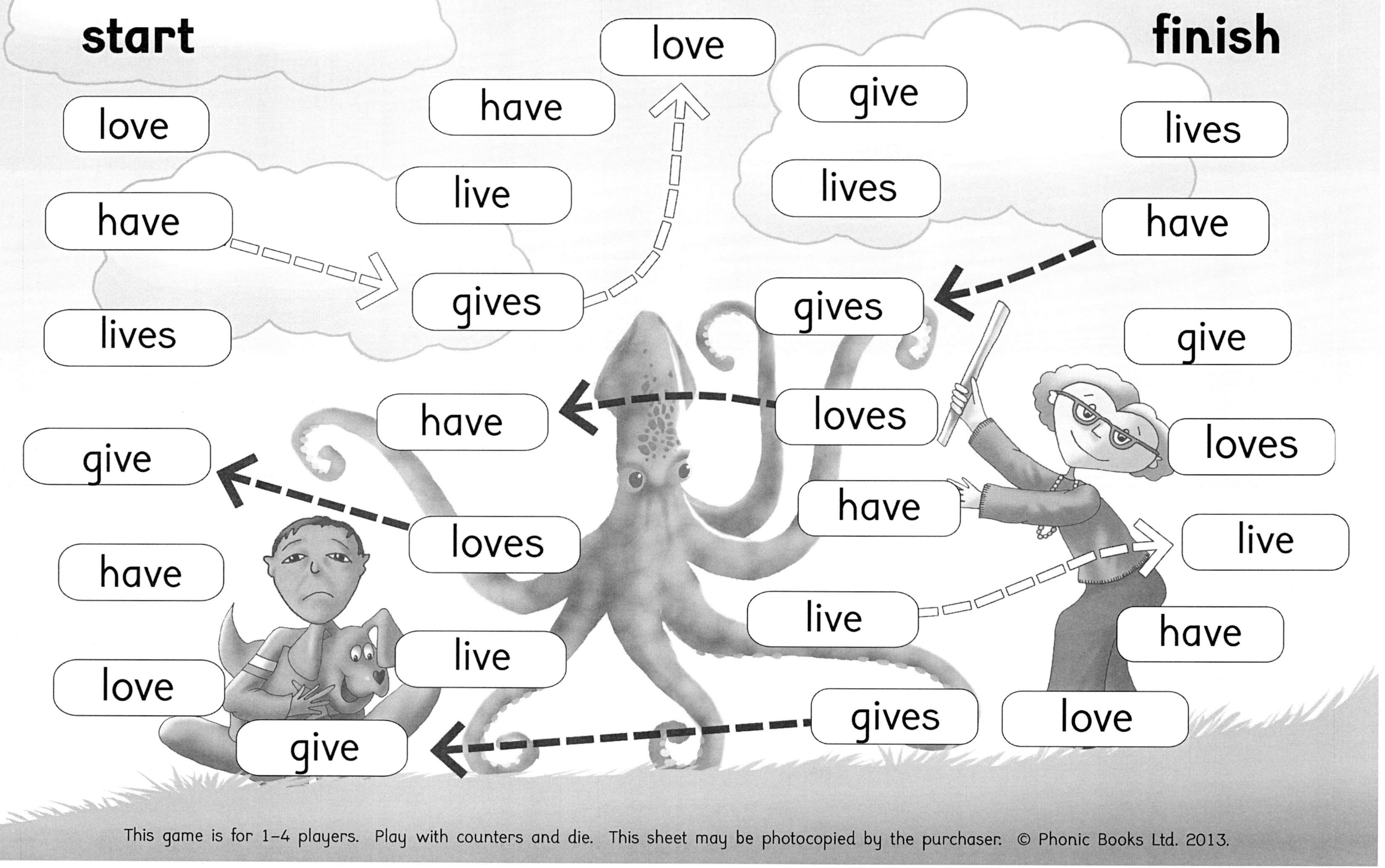

start — **finish**

love, have, lives, give, lives, gives, have, give, loves, loves, live, have
lives, have, live, gives, loves, have, live, gives, love
give, have, love, loves, live, give

This game is for 1–4 players. Play with counters and die. This sheet may be photocopied by the purchaser. © Phonic Books Ltd. 2013.

4-in-a-Row Game - Unit 16

this	long	have	along	they
her	loves	old	this	live
they	have	going	gives	long
loves	lives	with	have	loves
that	going	loves	they	old
gives	they	long	this	lives

Two different sets of coloured counters are needed. Two players take it in turns to read the word and put a counter on the word. The winner is the first to get four counters in a row. Play four games. When a game is won, the winner places a counter on the picture at the bottom of the page. This sheet may be photocopied by the purchaser. © Phonic Books Ltd 2013.

Lesson 17 – Unit 17

what

why

who

where

Unit 17 (1) - Find the word (1)

what ____ __ __	why ____ __
who ___ __	where ____

1. "____ __ is the lost dog?" " It is Meg, the pup."

2. "____ _____ am I? ____ _____ is Mum?" Meg thinks.

3. When Meg fell into the pond Dan said, " ____ __ __ a wet pup! ____ __ is this dog? I think the pup is lost!"

4. "____ __ is this?" asks Dad, "____ __ is he with you?"

Unit 17 spellings of high-frequency words, some of which have complex spellings: what, who, where, why. Explain that the letter <a> in the word <what> represents the sound 'o', the letters <wh> in the word <who> represent the sound 'h', the letter <o> in the word <who> represents the sound 'oo', the letters <ere> in the word <where> represent the sound 'air' and the letter <y> in the word <why> represents the sound 'ie'. Make sure the writer says the sounds as he/she writes the words. This sheet may be photocopied by the purchaser. © Phonic Books Ltd 2013.

Unit 17 (1) - Find the word (2)   107

what ____ __ __	why ____ __
who ____ __	where ____ _____

1. "You cannot have a dog," said Dad. "____ __ __ do you think Bob, the cat, will think?"

2. "____ __ is this dog?" thinks Bob. Bob is cross. "____ __ is this dog on my bed?"

3. "____ _____ can I sleep?" thinks Meg.

4. ____ __ is Bob in Meg's bed? Dan had got Meg a soft bed. Bob and Meg are pals. Meg lives with Bob and Dan.

Unit 17 spellings of high-frequency words, some of which have complex spellings: what, who, where, why. Explain that the letter <a> in the word <what> represents the sound 'o', the letters <wh> in the word <who> represent the sound 'h', the letter <o> in the word <who> represents the sound 'oo', the letters <ere> in the word <where> represent the sound 'air' and the letter <y> in the word <why> represents the sound 'ie'. Make sure the writer says the sounds as he/she writes the words. This sheet may be photocopied by the purchaser. © Phonic Books Ltd 2013.

108 Unit 17 (1) - Find the word - Teacher's sheet

| what | <u>wh</u> <u>a</u> <u>t</u> | why | <u>wh</u> <u>y</u> |
| who | <u>wh</u> <u>o</u> | where | <u>wh</u> <u>ere</u> |

Sheet 1

1. <u>Who</u> is the lost dog? It is Meg, the pup.

2. "<u>Where</u> am I? <u>Where</u> is Mum?" Meg thinks.

3. When Meg fell into the pond Dan said, "<u>What</u> a wet pup! <u>Who</u> is this dog? I think the pup is lost!"

4. "<u>Who</u> is this?" asks Dad, "<u>why</u> is he with you?"

Sheet 2

1. "You cannot have a dog," said Dad. "<u>What</u> do you think Bob, the cat, will think?"

2. "<u>Who</u> is this dog?" thinks Bob. Bob is cross. "<u>Why</u> is this dog on my bed?"

3. "<u>Where</u> can I sleep?" thinks Meg.

4. <u>Why</u> is Bob in Meg's bed? Dan had got Meg a soft bed. Bob and Meg are pals. Meg lives with Bob and Dan.

Unit 17 spellings of high-frequency words, some of which have complex spellings: what, who, where, why. Explain that the letter <a> in the word <what> represents the sound 'o', the letters <wh> in the word <who> represent the sound 'h', the letter <o> in the word <who> represents the sound 'oo', the letters <ere> in the word <where> represent the sound 'air' and the letter <y> in the word <why> represents the sound 'ie'. Make sure the writer says the sounds as he/she writes the words. This sheet may be photocopied by the purchaser. © Phonic Books Ltd 2013.

Unit 17 (2) - Find the word (1)

what ____ __ __	why ____ __
who ____ __	where ____ _____

1. "____ __ bit the jacket?" asks Dad. "____ __ bit the rug?" asks Dad. It is Meg. "____ __ __ a bad dog!" yells Dad.

2. Dad says Meg must go. "____ _____ must Meg go?" asks Dan. "Meg must live in the shed," says Dad.

3. Meg is upset. "____ __ must I live in the shed?"

4. "____ __ __ can I do?" thinks Dan. "____ __ can help Meg?" Then Dan has a plan. "____ __ don't I send Meg to a dog class?"

Unit 17 spellings of high-frequency words, some of which have complex spellings: what, who, where, why. Explain that the letter ‹a› in the word ‹what› represents the sound 'o', the letters ‹wh› in the word ‹who› represent the sound 'h', the letter ‹o› in the word ‹who› represents the sound 'oo', the letters ‹ere› in the word ‹where› represent the sound 'air' and the letter ‹y› in the word ‹why› represents the sound 'ie'. Make sure the writer says the sounds as he/she writes the words. This sheet may be photocopied by the purchaser. © Phonic Books Ltd 2013.

Unit 17 (2) - Find the word (2)

what ____ __ __	why ____ __
who ____ __	where ____ _____

1. Dan and Meg go to a dog class but Meg is bad. Meg does not sit, Meg does not run. "____ __ __ a bad dog!" says Dan.

2. ____ __ is at the dog class? It is Meg's pal, Will, the whippet. "You must be a good dog," says Will. "____ __ ?" asks Meg. "Then Dan's dad will let you back in," says Will.

3. "____ _____ is Dad?" says Dan. "Dad, look at Meg. Meg, sit!" Meg sits. "____ __ __ a good dog!" says Dad.

Unit 17 spellings of high-frequency words, some of which have complex spellings: what, who, where, why. Explain that the letter <a> in the word <what> represents the sound 'o', the letters <wh> in the word <who> represent the sound 'h', the letter <o> in the word <who> represents the sound 'oo', the letters <ere> in the word <where> represent the sound 'air' and the letter <y> in the word <why> represents the sound 'ie'. Make sure the writer says the sounds as he/she writes the words. This sheet may be photocopied by the purchaser. © Phonic Books Ltd 2013.

Unit 17 (2) – Find the word – Teacher's sheet

what	wh a t	why	wh y
who	wh o	where	wh ere

Sheet 1

1. "_Who_ bit the jacket?" asks Dad. "_Who_ bit the rug?" asks Dad. It is Meg. "_What_ a bad dog!" yells Dad.

2. Dad says Meg must go. "_Where_ must Meg go?" asks Dan. "Meg must live in the shed," says Dad.

3. Meg is upset. "_Why_ must I live in the shed?"

4. "_What_ can I do?" thinks Dan. "_Who_ can help Meg?" Then Dan has a plan. "_Why_ don't I send Meg to a dog class?"

Sheet 2

1. Dan and Meg go to a dog class but Meg is bad. Meg does not sit, Meg does not run. "_What_ a bad dog!" says Dan.

2. _Who_ is at the dog class? It is Meg's pal Will the whippet. "You must be a good dog," says Will. "_Why_?" asks Meg. "Then Dan's Dad will let you back in," says Will.

3. "_Where_ is Dad?" says Dan. "Dad, look at Meg. Meg, sit!" Meg sits. "_What_ a good dog!" says Dad.

Unit 17 spellings of high-frequency words, some of which have complex spellings: what, who, where, why. Explain that the letter <a> in the word <what> represents the sound 'o', the letters <wh> in the word <who> represent the sound 'h', the letter <o> in the word <who> represents the sound 'oo', the letters <ere> in the word <where> represent the sound 'air' and the letter <y> in the word <why> represents the sound 'ie'. Make sure the writer says the sounds as he/she writes the words. This sheet may be photocopied by the purchaser. © Phonic Books Ltd 2013.

Lesson 17
Stepping Stones game

start

finish

what, why, who, why, who, where, who, why, who, where, what, why, where, who, what, why, where, what, what, who, where, why, where, who, why, what, who, what, where

This game is for 1–4 players. Play with counters and die. This sheet may be photocopied by the purchaser. © Phonic Books Ltd. 2013.

4-in-a-Row Game – Unit 17

this	what	why	where	they
who	loves	old	this	who
they	why	going	what	long
loves	where	with	who	why
that	what	loves	they	where
where	they	who	this	what

Two different sets of coloured counters are needed. Two players take it in turns to read the word and put a counter on the word. The winner is the first to get four counters in a row. Play four games. When a game is won, the winner places a counter on the picture at the bottom of the page. This sheet may be photocopied by the purchaser. © Phonic Books Ltd 2013.

Lesson 18 – Unit 18

looked

into

asked

stopped

Unit 18 - Find the word (1)

looked __ ___ __ ___	into __ __ __ __
asked __ __ __ ___	stopped __ __ __ ___ ___

1. The clock rang. Sam __ ___ __ ___ at the clock.

   It was 12 o'clock. Sam __ __ __ ___ ___ the clock.

2. Sam tapped Tam and __ __ __ ___ Tam to get up.

   She __ ___ __ ___ at Sam, blinked and got up.

3. Sam and Tam crept down the steps. Tam

   __ ___ __ ___ __ __ __ __ the tin to grab a

   bun but dropped the tin. "Shhh!" said Sam.

4. Sam __ ___ __ ___ for milk.

   He put milk __ __ __ __

   a cup and spilt it.

Unit 18 spellings of high-frequency words, some of which have complex spellings: looked, stopped, asked, into. Explain that the letters <oo> in the word <into> represent the sound /oo/ and the letter <o> in the word <into> has the sound /oo/ as in <moon>. Make sure the writer says the sounds as he/she writes the words. This sheet may be photocopied by the purchaser. © Phonic Books Ltd 2013.

Unit 18 - Find the word (2)

| looked __ ____ __ ____ | into __ __ __ __ |
| asked __ __ __ ____ | stopped __ __ __ ____ |

1. "Shall we have some crisps?" __ __ __ ____ Sam.

   He ripped the pack and spilt the crisps.

2. Then Mum and Dad rushed in. "What is this mess?". __ __ __ ____ Dad.

3. Dan is trapped in the chest.

   Raj and Liz __ ____ __ ____ for Dan.

   Meg __ __ __ ____ ____ next to the chest.

   Liz lifted the lid and __ ____ __ ____

   __ __ __ __ the chest. Dan jumped up. Meg did well to find Dan.

Unit 18 spellings of high-frequency words, some of which have complex spellings: looked, stopped, asked, into. Explain that the letters <oo> in the word <into> represent the sound /oo/ and the letter <o> in the word <into> has the sound /oo/ as in <moon>. Make sure the writer says the sounds as he/she writes the words. This sheet may be photocopied by the purchaser. © Phonic Books Ltd 2013.

Unit 18 - Find the word – Teacher's sheet

looked	l *oo* k ed	into	i n t o
asked	a s k ed	stopped	s t o pp ed

Sheet 1

1. The clock rang. Sam *looked* at the clock. It was 12 o'clock. Sam *stopped* the clock.

2. Sam tapped Tam and *asked* Tam to get up. She *looked* at Sam, blinked and got up.

3. Sam and Tam crept down the steps. Tam *looked into* the tin and grabbed a bun. Tam dropped the tin.

4. Sam *looked* for milk. He put milk *into* a cup and spilt it.

Sheet 2

1. "Shall we have some crisps?" *asked* Sam. He ripped the pack and spilt the crisps.

2. Then Mum and Dad rushed in.
   "What is this mess?" *asked* Dad.

3. Dan is trapped in the chest.
   Raj and Liz *looked* for Dan.
   Meg *stopped* next to the chest.
   Liz lifted the lid and *looked into* the chest.
   Dan jumped up. Meg did well to find Dan.

Unit 18 spellings of high-frequency words, some of which have complex spellings: looked, stopped, asked, into. Explain that the letters <oo> in the word <into> represent the sound /oo/ and the letter <o> in the word <into> has the sound /oo/ as in <moon>. Make sure the writer says the sounds as he/she writes the words. This sheet may be photocopied by the purchaser. © Phonic Books Ltd 2013.

Lesson 18
Stepping Stones game

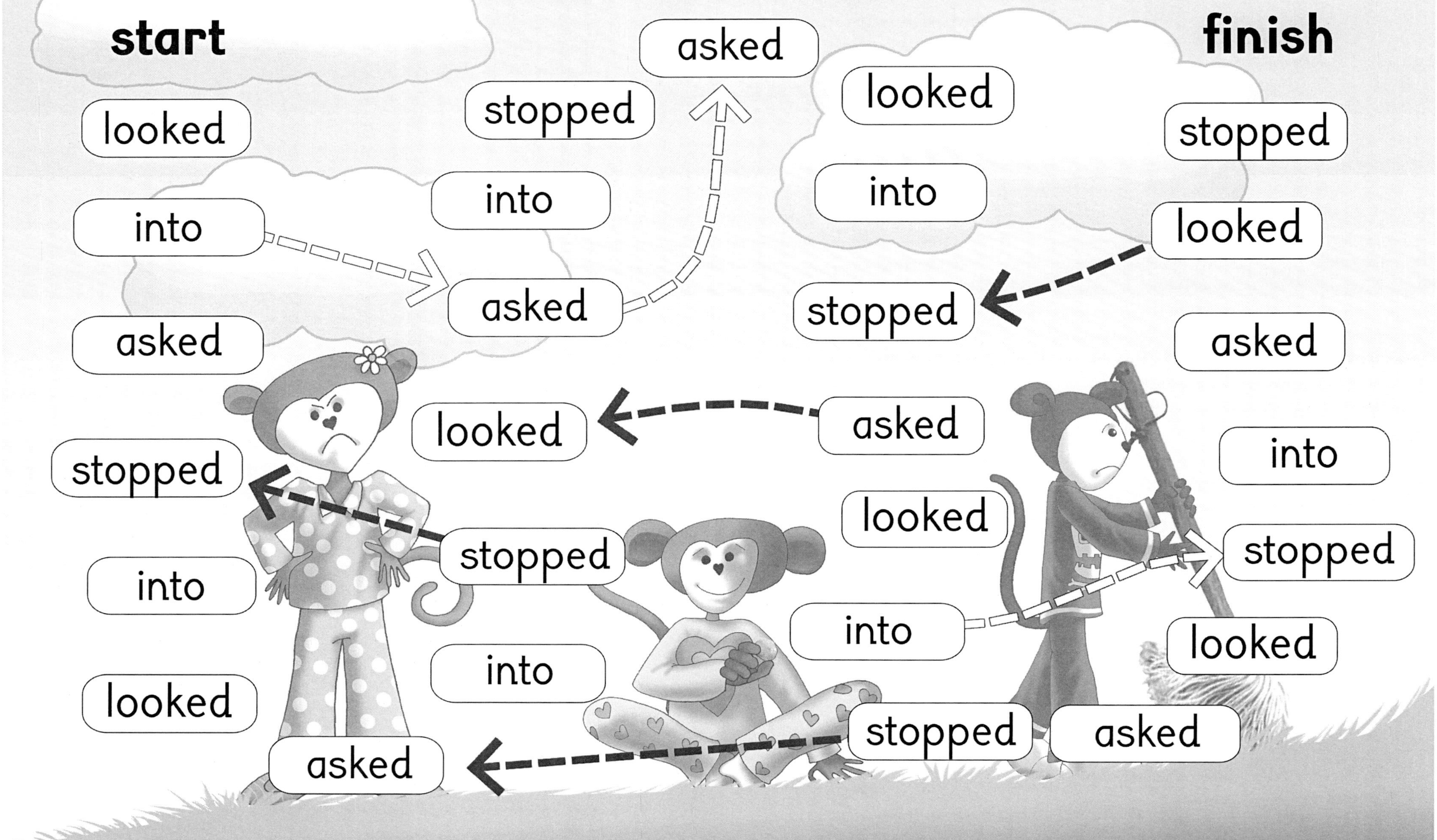

start

finish

looked — into — asked — stopped — into — asked — looked — stopped — asked — looked — into — stopped

looked — into — asked — stopped — into — looked — stopped — asked — looked — into — stopped — asked — looked

This game is for 1–4 players. Play with counters and die. This sheet may be photocopied by the purchaser. © Phonic Books Ltd. 2013.

4-in-a-Row-Game - Unit 18

why	what	where	into	they
who	asked	looked	stopped	who
they	why	into	what	asked
asked	where	stopped	who	why
looked	what	loves	they	where
where	they	who	stopped	what

Two different sets of coloured counters are needed. Two players take it in turns to read the word and put a counter on the word. The winner is the first to get four counters in a row. Play four games. When a game is won, the winner places a counter on the picture at the bottom of the page. This sheet may be photocopied by the purchaser. © Phonic Books Ltd 2013.

Lesson 19 – Unit 19

too

all

by

began

Unit 19 - Find the word (1)

too __ ____	all __ ____
by __ __	began __ __ __ __ __

1. Chen, Liz and Raj packed a bag. They __ ____ went for a picnic __ __ a big pond.

2. Chen was standing on quicksand when he __ __ __ __ __ to sink.

3. Raj went to help Chen and he __ __ __ __ __ to sink __ ____.

4. "Hold onto this branch," said Liz. Then they __ ____ sat __ __ the pond and had a picnic sitting on a patch of grass.

Unit 19 spellings of high-frequency words, some of which have complex spellings: too, all, by, began. Explain that the letters <oo> in the word <too> represent the sound /oo/, the letter <a> in the word <all> represents the sound /or/, the letter <y> in the word <by> represents the sound /ie/ and the letter <e> in the word <began> represents the sound /ee/. Make sure the writer says the sounds as he/she writes the words. This sheet may be photocopied by the purchaser. © Phonic Books Ltd 2013.

Unit 19 - Find the word (2)   123

| too __ ____ | all __ ____ |
| by __ __ | began __ __ __ __ __ |

1. Wilf __ __ __ __ __ to nod off __ __ the pond.

   Wilf's dust was in a bag __ __ him.

2. Dan had a wish. __ ____ of a sudden, he

   __ __ __ __ __ to shrink and was sitting

   __ __ a frog in the pond.

3. Dan jumped into the pond.

   The frog jumped in __ ____.

4. __ ____ the fish began to swim from Dan and the

   frog. "The fish are cross and I am cross __ ____!"

   said Wilf. "Elf dust is not for kids!"

Unit 19 spellings of high-frequency words, some of which have complex spellings: too, all, by, began. Explain that the letters <oo> in the word <too> represent the sound /oo/, the letter <a> in the word <all> represents the sound /or/, the letter <y> in the word <by> represents the sound /ie/ and the letter <e> in the word <began> represents the sound /ee/. Make sure the writer says the sounds as he/she writes the words. This sheet may be photocopied by the purchaser. © Phonic Books Ltd 2013.

Unit 19 - Find the word – Teacher's sheet

too	<u>t</u> <u>oo</u>	all	<u>a</u> <u>ll</u>
by	<u>b</u> <u>y</u>	began	<u>b</u> <u>e</u> <u>g</u> <u>a</u> <u>n</u>

Sheet 1

1- Chen, Liz and Raj packed a bag. They <u>all</u> went for a picnic <u>by</u> a big pond.

2- Chen was standing on quicksand when he <u>began</u> to sink.

3- Raj went to help Chen and he <u>began</u> to sink <u>too</u>.

4- "Hold onto this branch," said Liz. Then they <u>all</u> sat <u>by</u> the pond and had a picnic sitting on a patch of grass.

Sheet 2

5- Wilf <u>began</u> to nod off <u>by</u> the pond. Wilf's dust was in a bag <u>by</u> him.

6- Dan had a wish. <u>All</u> of a sudden, he <u>began</u> to shrink and was sitting <u>by</u> a frog in the pond.

7- Dan jumped into the pond. The frog jumped in <u>too</u>.

8- <u>All</u> the fish began to swim from Dan and the frog. "The fish are cross and I am cross <u>too</u>!" said Wilf. "Elf dust is not for kids."

Unit 19 spellings of high-frequency words, some of which have complex spellings: too, all, by, began. Explain that the letters <oo> in the word <too> represent the sound /oo/, the letter <a> in the word <all> represents the sound /or/, the letter <y> in the word <by> represents the sound /ie/ and the letter <e> in the word <began> represents the sound /ee/. Make sure the writer says the sounds as he/she writes the words. This sheet may be photocopied by the purchaser. © Phonic Books Ltd 2013.

Lesson 19
Stepping Stones game

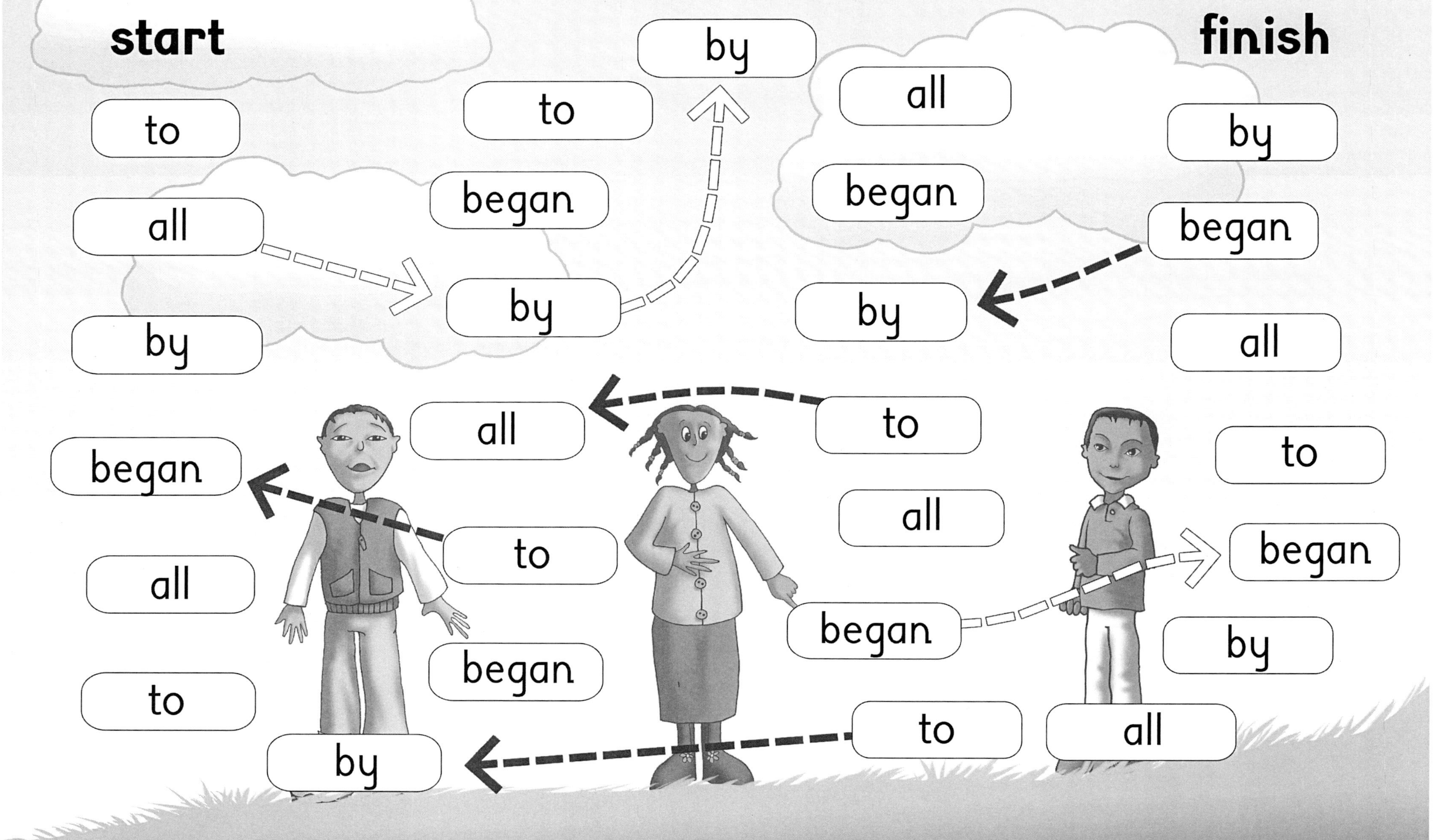

start — to, all, by, began, all, by, to, all, began, by, to, all, began, by, all, to, began, by, all, to, by, began, all, **finish**

This game is for 1–4 players. Play with counters and die. This sheet may be photocopied by the purchaser. © Phonic Books Ltd. 2013.

4-in-a-Row Game - Unit 19

why	what	where	began	they
who	too	looked	all	who
they	why	by	what	began
too	began	all	who	why
looked	by	loves	they	where
where	too	who	all	what

Two different sets of coloured counters are needed. Two players take it in turns to read the word and put a counter on the word. The winner is the first to get four counters in a row. Play four games. When a game is won, the winner places a counter on the picture at the bottom of the page. This sheet may be photocopied by the purchaser. © Phonic Books Ltd 2013.

Lesson 20 - Unit 20

once

oh

one

there

Unit 20 - Find the word (1)

| once _____ | oh ____ |
| one _____ | there ____ _____ |

1. _____, mum left an apple crumble ____ _____, on the top.

2. Pip and Tess smelt the apple crumble. "____! My tum is rumbling and grumbling all at _____!" said Pip.

3. ____ _____ it is on the top," said Pip.

4. Let us have _____ little nibble!" said Tess.

5. _____ Pip had had a little nibble he said, "It is too hot!"

Unit 20 spellings of high-frequency words, some of which have complex spellings: oh, there, one, once. Explain that the letters <oh> in the word <oh> represent the sound /oe/ and the letters <ere> in the word <there> represent the sound /air/. The words <one> and <once> need to be learnt as special words. It can be pointed out that the <ce> in <once> represents the /s/ sound. Make sure the writer says the sounds as he/she writes the words except for <one> and <once> This sheet may be photocopied by the purchaser. © Phonic Books Ltd 2013.

Unit 20 - Find the word (2)

> once _____   oh ____
>
> one _____   there ____ _____

1. ____ no! Pip wobbled _____ and then tumbled into the crumble. It was hot.

2. Then Pip was swept up by a kid and tipped into a dish, ____ _____, on the table.

3. The kid saw _____ little ant, ____ _____ , in his crumble.

4. "____ no! Not an ant in my crumble," said the kid. He picked up Pip and let him go.

Unit 20 spellings of high-frequency words, some of which have complex spellings: oh, there, one, once. Explain that the letters <oh> in the word <oh> represent the sound /oe/ and the letters <ere> in the word <there> represent the sound /air/. The words <one> and <once> need to be learnt as special words. It can be pointed out that the <ce> in <once> represents the /s/ sound. Make sure the writer says the sounds as he/she writes the words except for <one> and <once> This sheet may be photocopied by the purchaser. © Phonic Books Ltd 2013.

Unit 20 - Find the word – Teacher's sheet

once _once_	oh _a ll_
one _one_	there _th ere_

Sheet 1

1. _Once_, mum left an apple crumble _there_, on the top.
2. Pip and Tess smelt the apple crumble. "_Oh!_ My tum is rumbling and grumbling all at _once!_" said Pip.
3. "_There_ it is on the top," said Pip.
4. "Let us have _one_ little nibble!" said Tess.
5. _Once_ Pip had had a little nibble he said, "It is too hot!"

Sheet 2

1. Oh no! Pip wobbled _once_ and then tumbled into the crumble. It was hot!
2. Then Pip was swept up by a kid and tipped into a dish, _there_, on the table.
3. The kid saw _one_ little ant, _there_, in his crumble.
4. "_Oh_, no! Not an ant in my crumble," said the kid. He picked Pip up and let him go.

Unit 20 spellings of high-frequency words, some of which have complex spellings: oh, there, one, once. Explain that the letters <oh> in the word <oh> represent the sound /oe/ and the letters <ere> in the word <there> represent the sound /air/. The words <one> and <once> need to be learnt as special words. It can be pointed out that the <ce> in <once> represents the /s/ sound. Make sure the writer says the sounds as he/she writes the words except for <one> and <once> This sheet may be photocopied by the purchaser. © Phonic Books Ltd 2013.

Lesson 20
Stepping Stones game

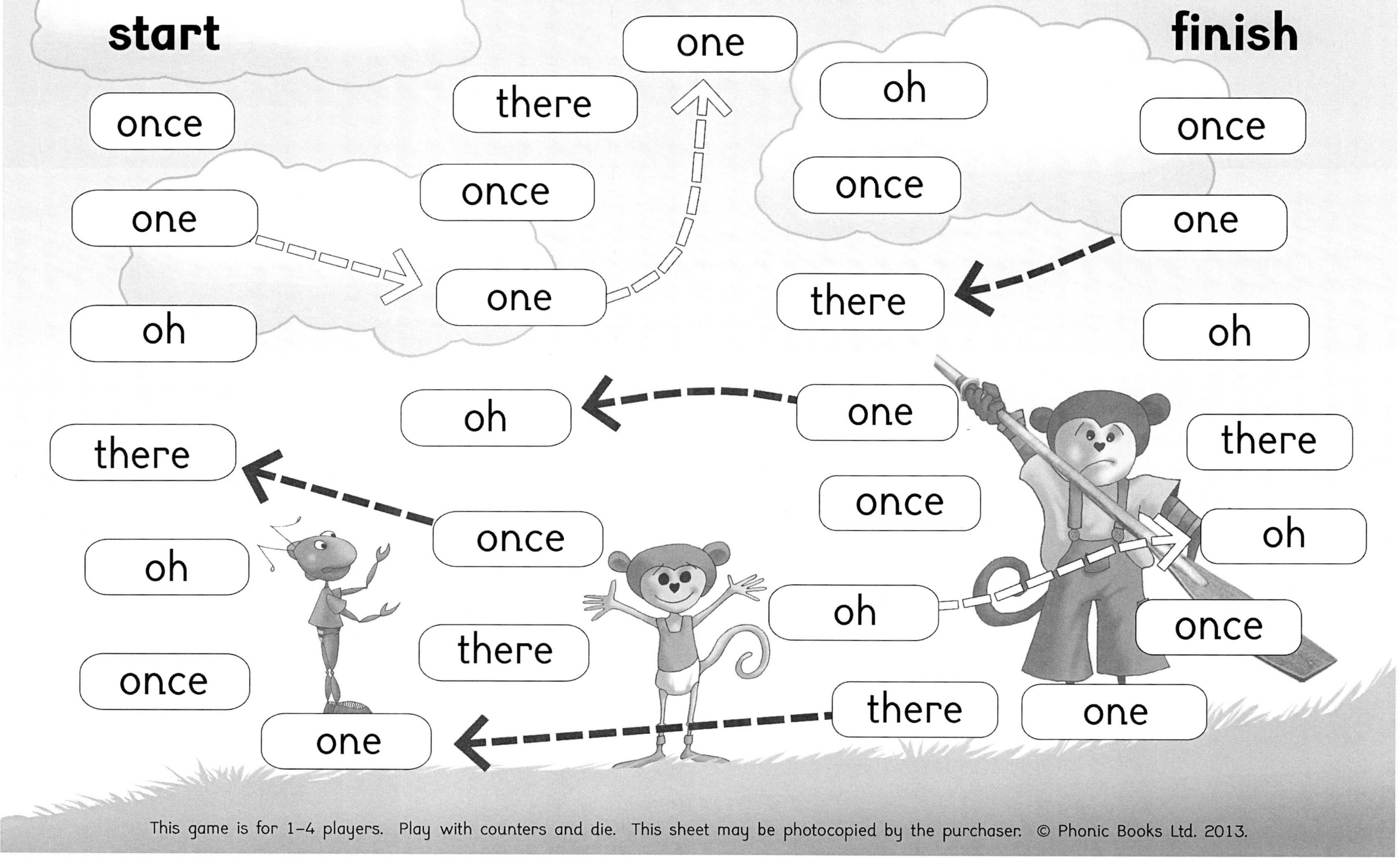

start

finish

once, one, oh, there, oh, once, one, there

oh, once, there, one, once, oh, there

one, there, once, one

once, one, oh, there, oh, once

This game is for 1–4 players. Play with counters and die. This sheet may be photocopied by the purchaser. © Phonic Books Ltd. 2013.

4 in-a-Row Game - Lesson 20

why	what	where	once	all
who	one	looked	there	who
they	all	oh	what	began
there	once	one	who	oh
one	by	all	once	where
where	one	who	oh	what

Two different sets of coloured counters are needed. Two players take it in turns to read the word and put a counter on the word. The winner is the first to get four counters in a row. Play four games. When a game is won, the winner places a counter on the picture at the bottom of the page. This sheet may be photocopied by the purchaser. © Phonic Books Ltd 2013.

Lesson 1 – Unit 1

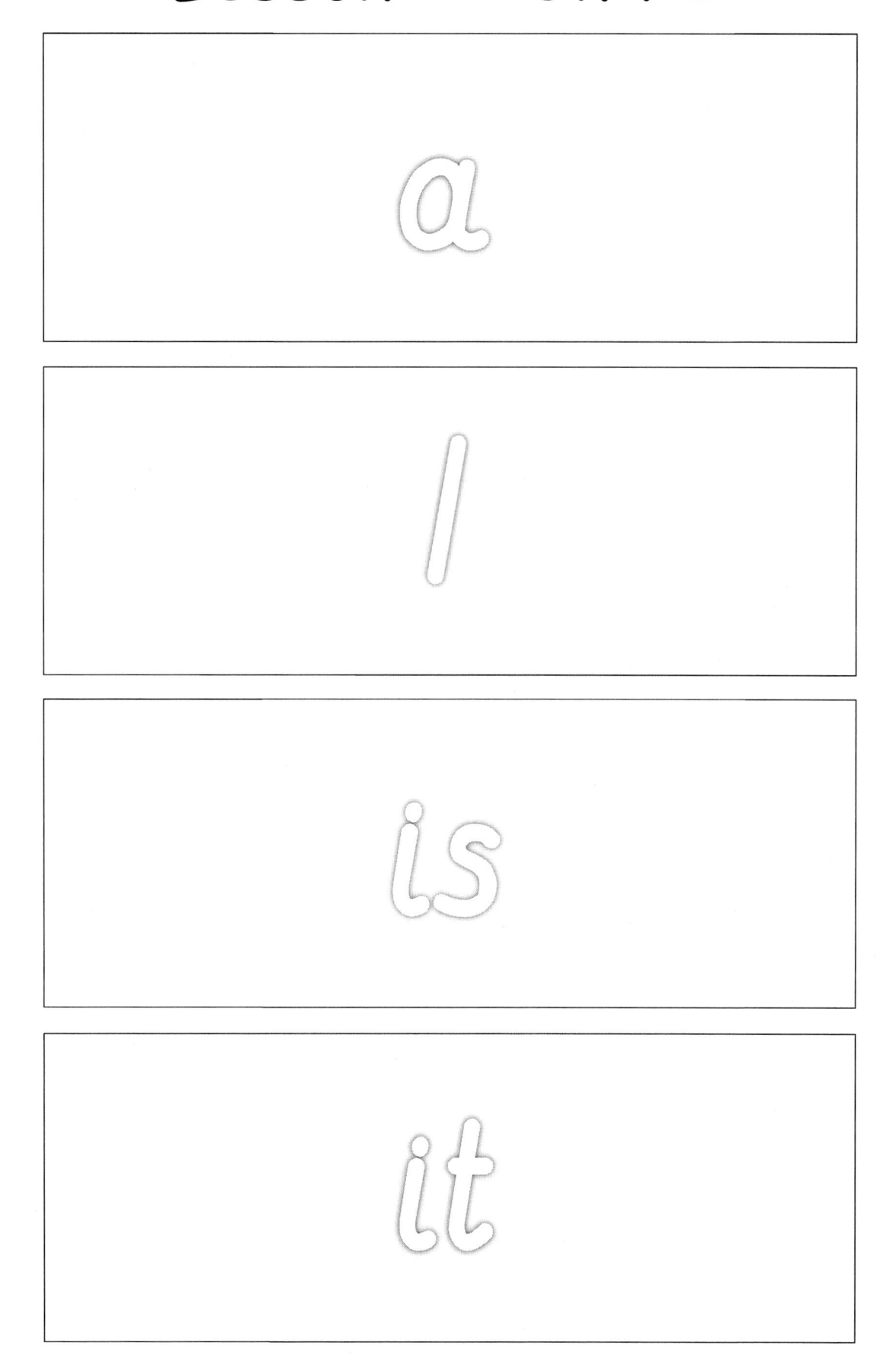

a

I

is

it

Lesson 2 – Unit 2

the

not

is

on

Lesson 3 - Unit 3

his

has

can

the

This page may be photocopied by the purchaser. © Phonic Books Ltd 2013..

Lesson 4 – Unit 4

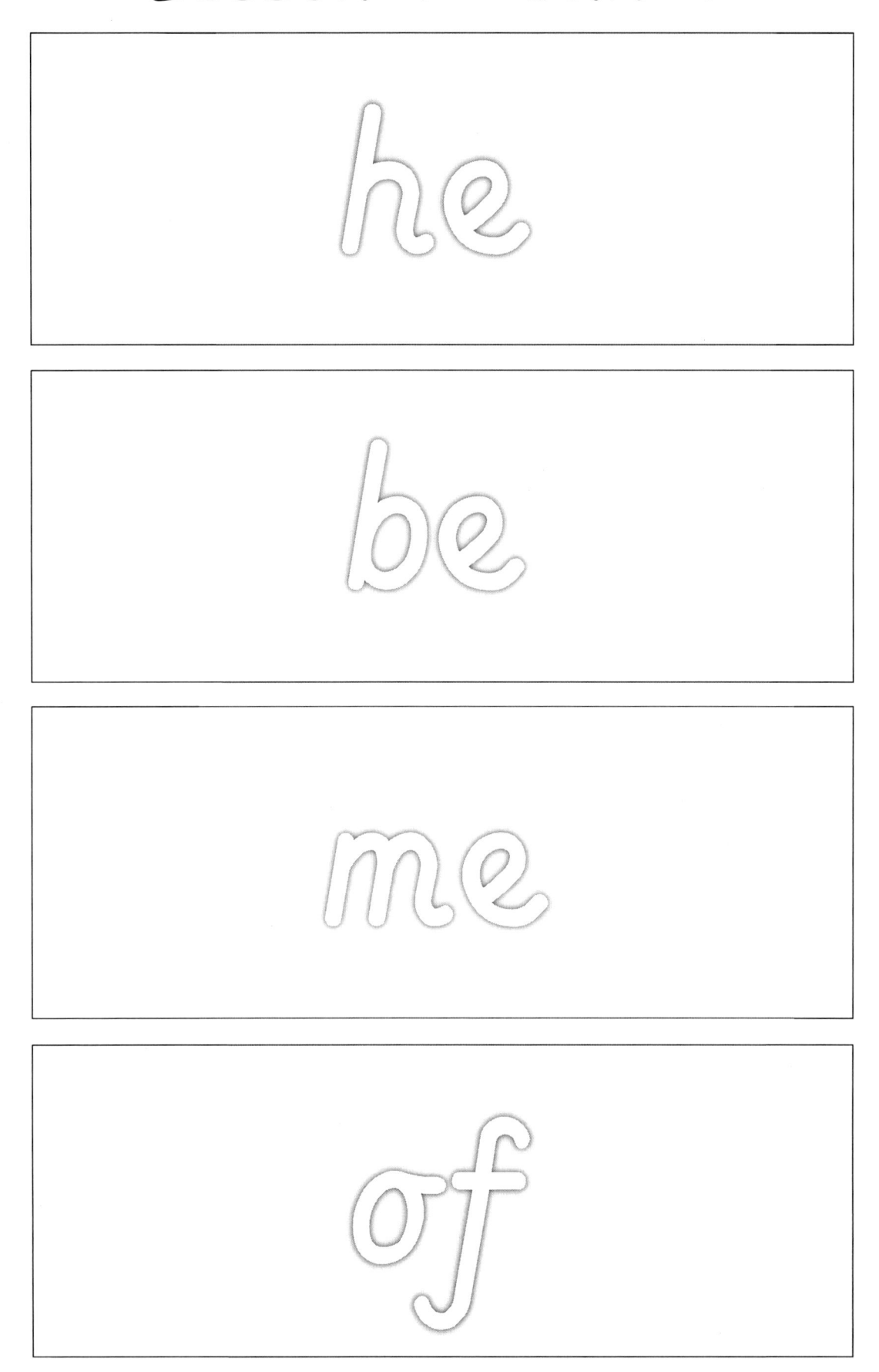

he

be

me

of

Lesson 5 - Unit 5

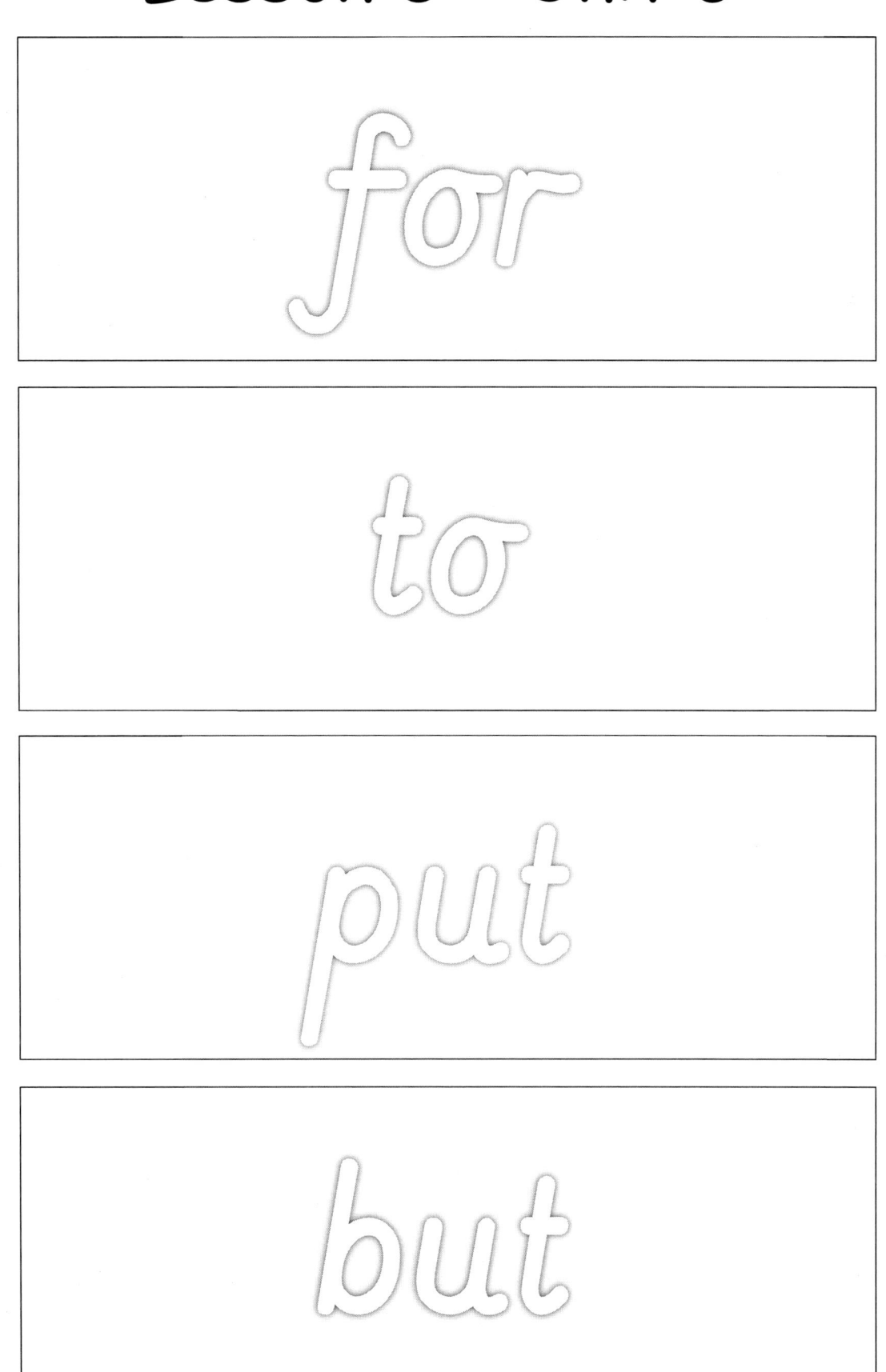

for

to

put

but

Lesson 6 – Unit 6

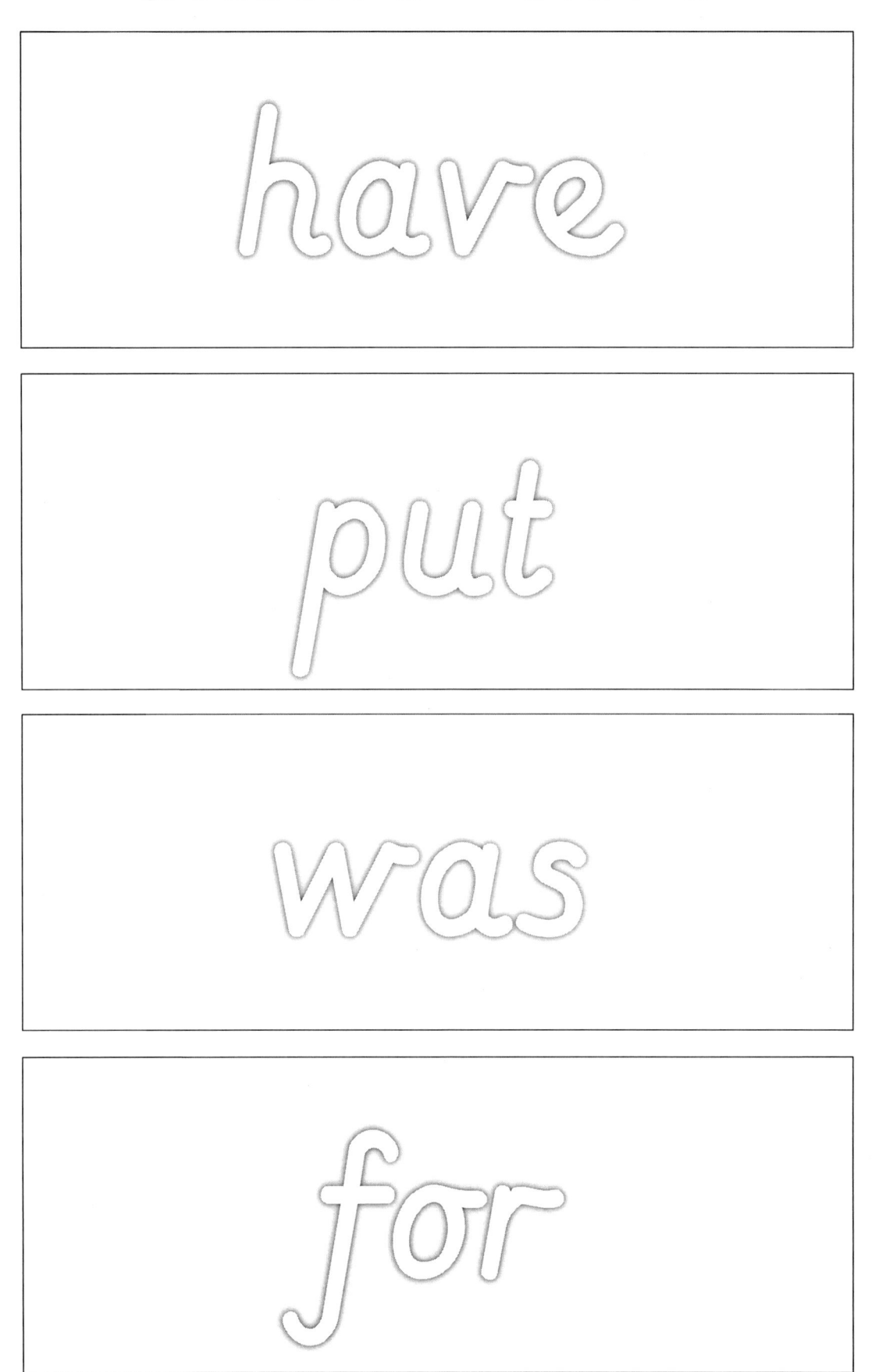

| have |

| put |

| was |

| for |

Lesson 7 – Unit 7

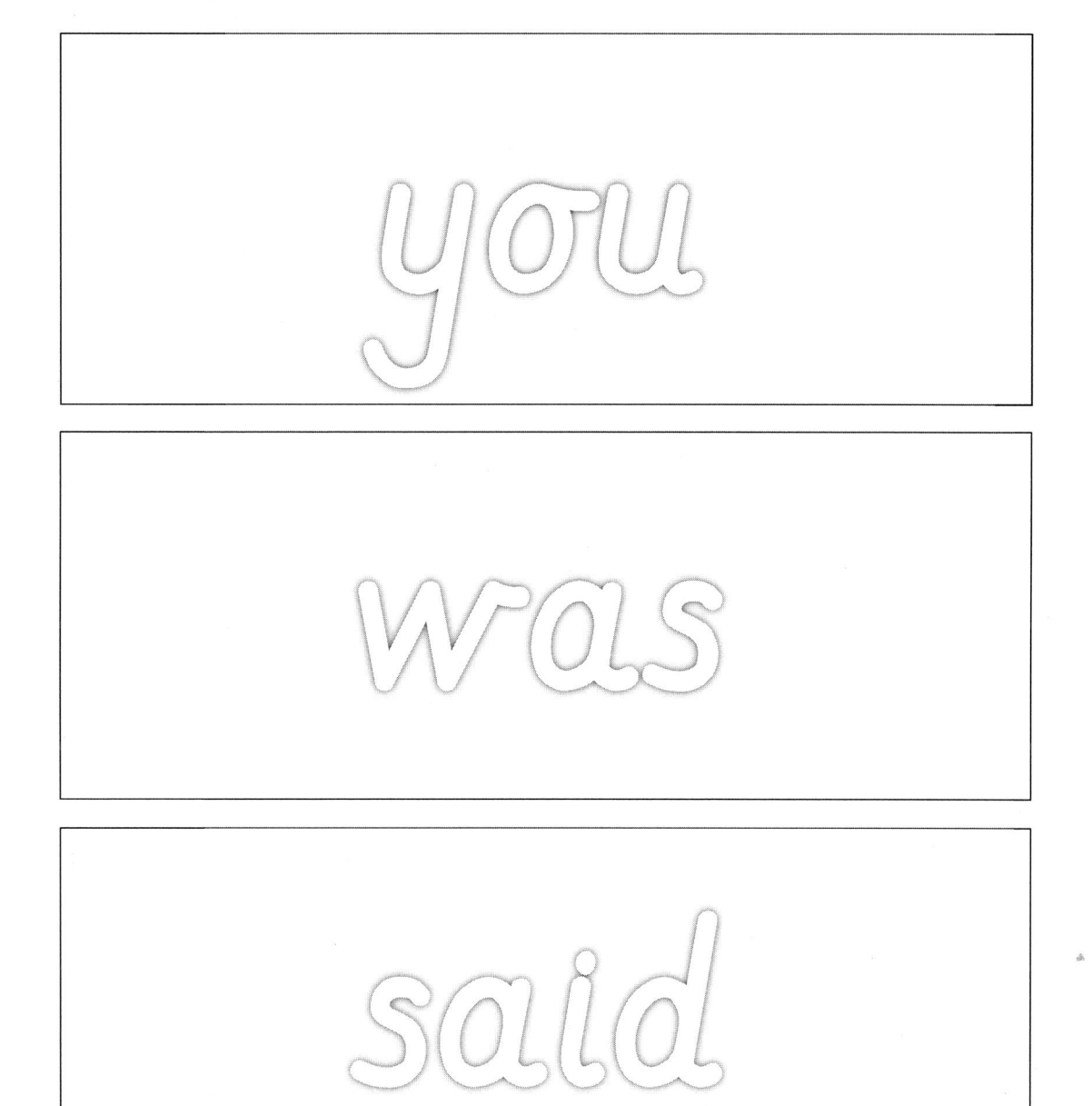

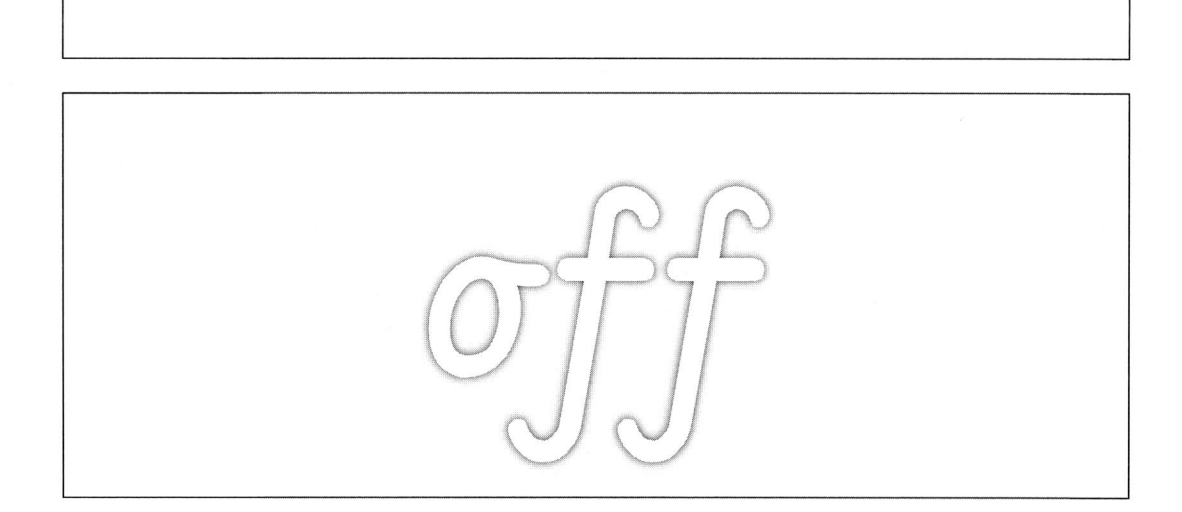

you

was

said

off

Lesson 8 – Unit 8

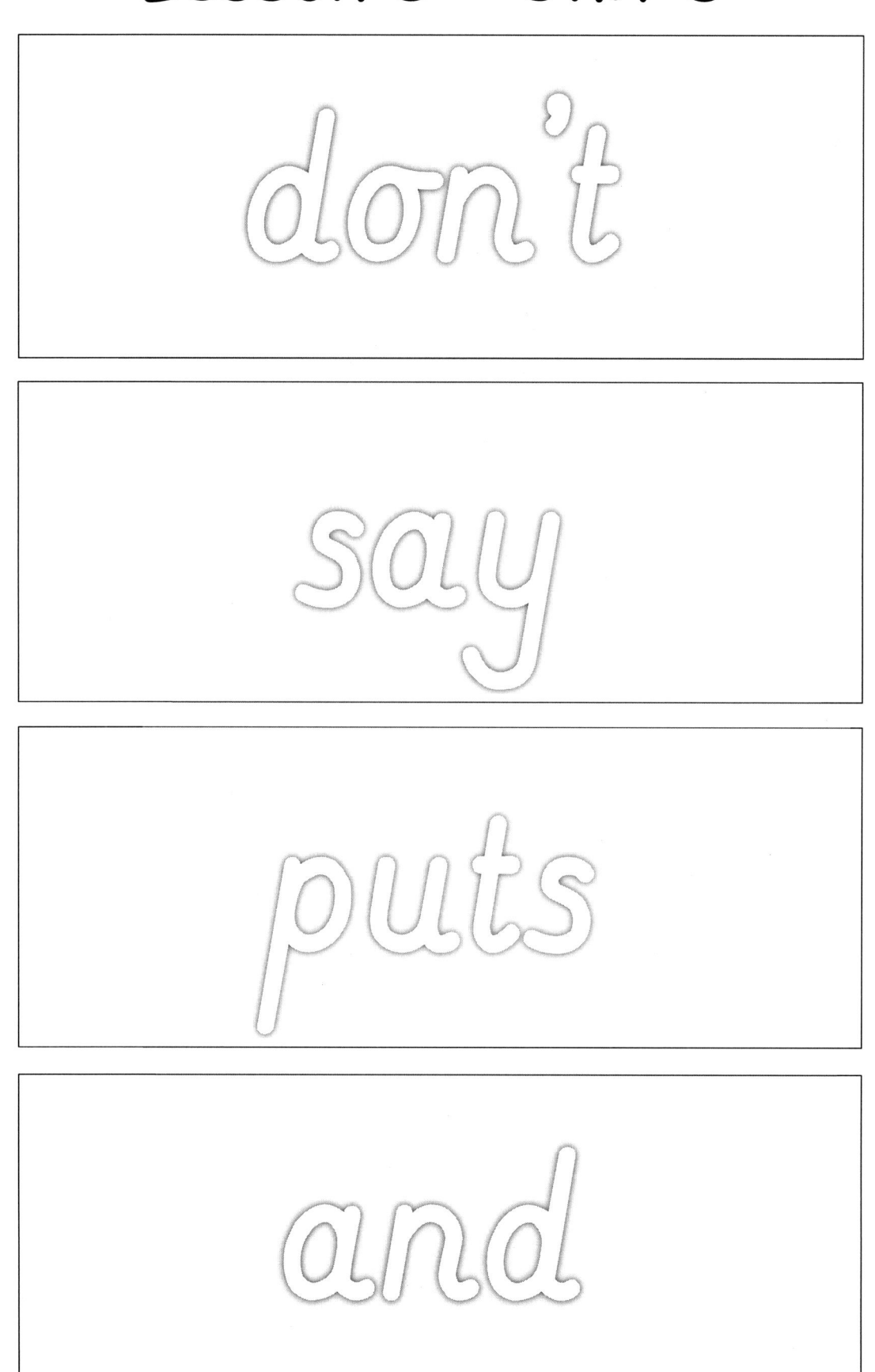

don't

say

puts

and

Lesson 9 – Unit 9

do

says

from

are

Lesson 10 – Unit 10

don't

says

love

my

Lesson 11 - Unit 11

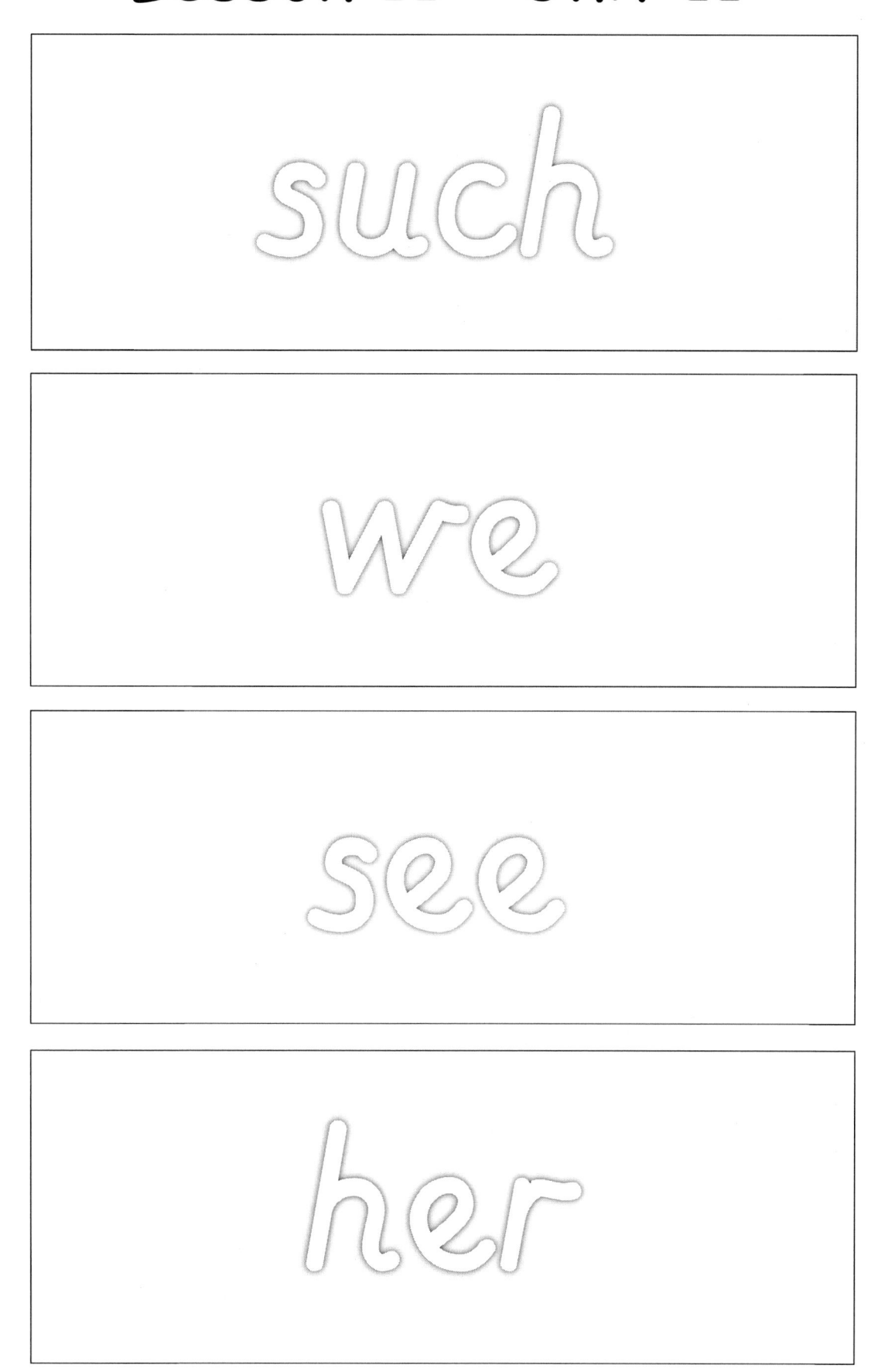

such

we

see

her

Lesson 12 – Unit 12

she

wish

give

live

Lesson 13 - Unit 13

this

that

they

with

Lesson 14 – Unit 14

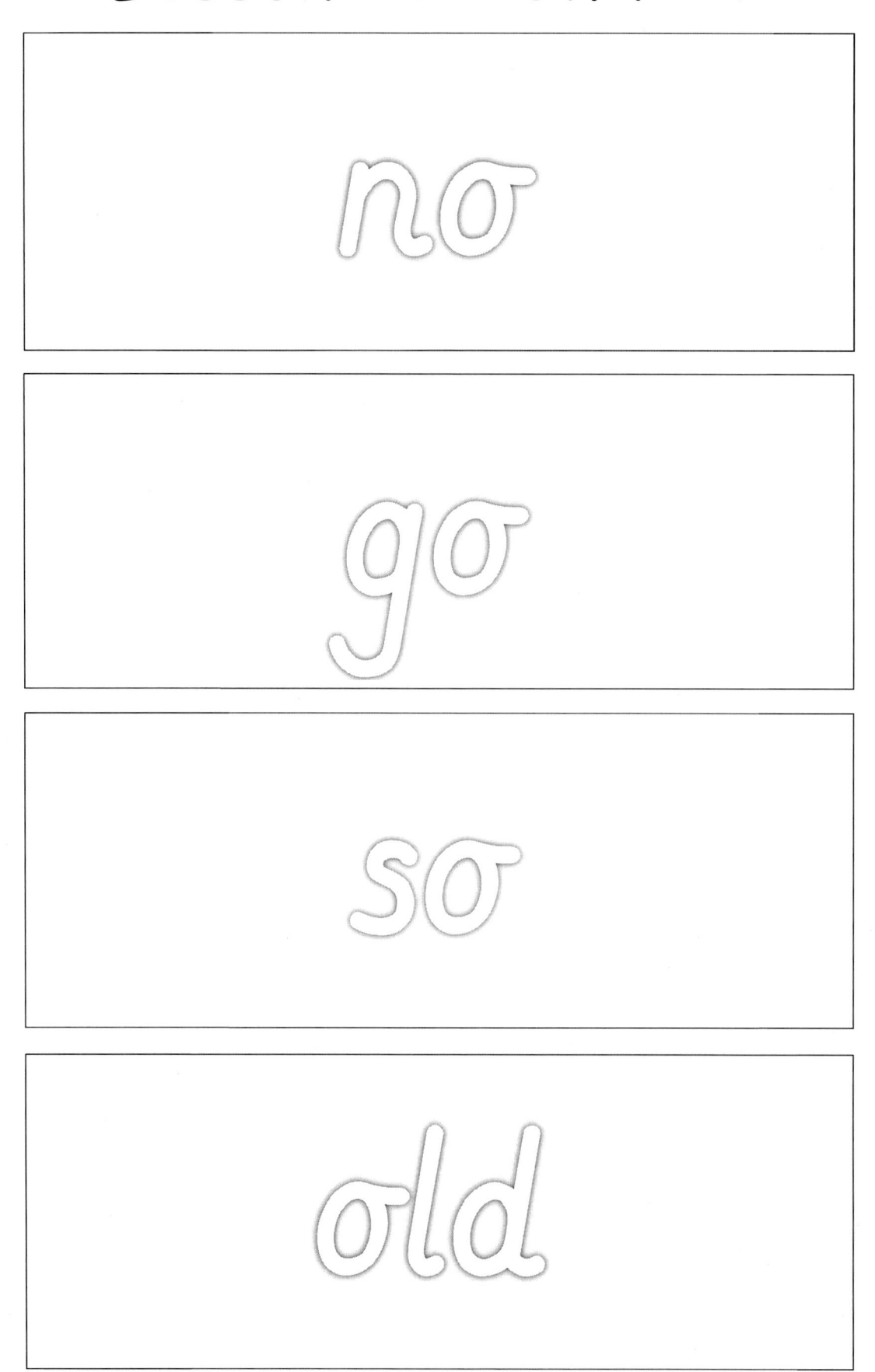

no

go

so

old

Lesson 15 - Unit 15

long

along

going

think

Lesson 16 – Unit 16

loves

have

lives

gives

Lesson 17 – Unit 17

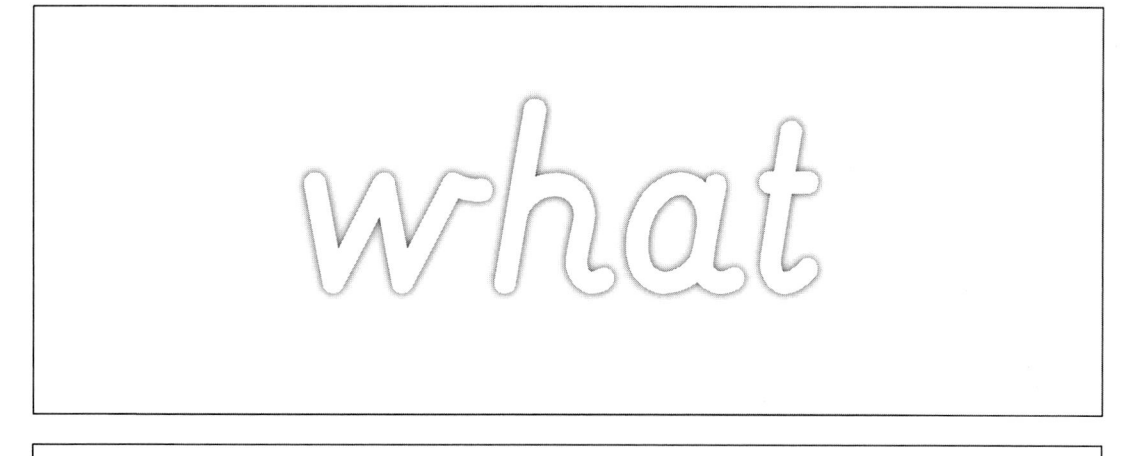

what

why

who

where

Lesson 18 – Unit 18

looked

into

asked

stopped

Lesson 19 - Unit 19

too

all

by

began

Lesson 20 – Unit 20

once

oh

one

there